GROWING IN FAITH

GROWING IN FAITH

A Guide for the
Reluctant Christian

DAVID YOUNT

Foreword by Lord Donald Coggan
101st Archbishop of Canterbury

REGNERY PUBLISHING, INC.

Washington, D.C.

Library of Congress Cataloging-in-Publication Data

Yount, David.
Growing in faith : a guide for the reluctant Christian /
David Yount ; foreword by Lord Donald Coggan.
p.   cm.
Includes index.
ISBN 0-89526-494-3 (alk. paper)
1. Faith.   2. Theology, Doctrinal.   3. Christian life—Catholic
authors.   I. Title.
BT771.2.Y68   1994
239—dc20   94-529
CIP

Published in the United States by
Regnery Publishing, Inc.
An Eagle Publishing, Inc. Company
422 First St., SE, Suite 300
Washington, DC 20003

Distributed to the trade by
National Book Network
4720-A Boston Way
Lanham, MD 20706

Printed on acid-free paper.

Manufactured in the United States of America.

10 9 8 7 6 5 4 3 2

For my wife

. . . for the sake of Rebecca
because she was fair to look upon.
Genesis 26:7

This small book is dedicated, as well, to all those men and women of good will who consider themselves Christians but who, for whatever reason, are unsure of their beliefs or are alienated from the faith of their childhood.

It is also dedicated to the millions of church-going Christians whose faith was formed and informed in childhood but is stuck there—inadequate to confront the challenges of adulthood.

CONTENTS

FOREWORD

William Temple, one of the greatest of the archbishops of Canterbury, used to say that many clergy were expert at answering questions which the average lay person never asked. There is enough truth in that saying to make many preachers and authors uneasy.

David Yount has a deep concern to meet ordinary lay people where they actually are and to help them with the questions which truly perplex them. That is the reason for this book. Because I share the author's concern, and because I believe this book is likely to help many, I am glad to commend the book.

When I have found myself disagreeing with views expressed and putting question marks in the margin of the typescript, I have reminded myself of the words of the dedication: the book is for those who "are unsure of their beliefs or are alienated from the faith of their childhood" and for those "whose faith was formed and informed in childhood but is stuck there." Their number is legion; and I believe God's heart goes out to them. Clearly the author's does. So does mine.

David Yount calls it "a small book." Maybe, but it covers

a vast area. That is a measure of the author's daring. The book will arouse further questions; that is what it is meant to do. But it will also prick consciences; "Ay, there's the rub," as Shakespeare wrote. But a rub can lead to healing, a wound to wholeness. In that deep sense, I wish the book well. May it flourish.

Lord Donald Coggan
101st Archbishop of Canterbury

PREFACE:
A RELUCTANCE TO BELIEVE

An international poll taken in 1993 revealed that only two of every one hundred Americans have no belief in God and that another four are unsure about God's existence—leaving 94 percent of Americans believers of some sort. Ironically, only one other place in the world, bloody Northern Ireland, matches this extraordinary statistic of religious belief.

As Christianity celebrates nearly two thousand years of faith, half of all Americans still worship in a church every week of the year. Nevertheless, religion is routinely ignored, denigrated, or condemned by the media and popular culture in the United States. When cult leader David Koresh precipitated an apocalyptic conclusion to his life and those of his followers in 1993 by torching their Texas colony, one reporter characterized the tragedy as proving that "there's no nut like a religious nut."

Despite these negative generalizations thrown about so casually, the majority of Americans cannot conceive of being anything but Christian. Ours is, after all, a young nation with a persistent Christian heritage drawn from many cultures. Despite separation of church and state, Christian symbols abound even in public life. The common penny proclaims, "In God we trust." In our nation's capital, where I toil, most of the architecture is classical, suggestive of those great civilizations of ancient Greece and Rome, but upon reading the inscriptions on the buildings and the monuments no one can mistake Washington, D.C., for a polytheistic Athens or pagan Rome.

Perhaps you are a man or woman moving among that vast majority of believers who acknowledge God's existence, yet you shy away from the consequences and commitments implicit in your faith for fear that they may be more than you can handle and will only expose your shortcomings. You may have lapsed from the practice of your religion or turned from the church in anger. You may have felt driven away or abandoned. Nevertheless, you still believe; you know that people without faith flounder.

If you are such a person, you are a reluctant Christian. You believe in God because you cannot conceive of a world without a Creator who sustains it. And even if you are a church-goer, you may be the sort who tries to live a responsible life armed with a faith that has not developed beyond childhood. You may be easily put off by Christians who claim to be absolutely certain of their faith. You may suspect that much of what other people profess is superstition. You may be skeptical of popes and preachers and inclined to believe that the church meddles too much in politics and people's lives. Although you find Jesus attractive, you perceive him to be strange and a little forbidding. You would like to know more because you want to be clear about the purpose of life and your place in it, but you hesitate to allow religion to dominate your life.

Occasionally you may indulge yourself excessively or fly off the handle, but you are no great sinner. Rather, you are convinced that there are good things you could be doing with your life if you could only focus more clearly, gain perspective, establish priorities, husband your energies, and dedicate your life. You can't conceive of Bible reading taking the place of television in your life, and you are an unlikely candidate to sing in a church choir. But you want to be respected for what you believe and what you are, and have it reflected in the memories of your loved ones when you eventually depart this life. It is important to be known as a person of conviction; but to take a stand you need a faith to stand on.

Congratulations and welcome: you have found the right book. Rest assured that I will not preach at or patronize you. What I can offer you in these pages is a better knowledge of the Christian faith that may allay some of your reluctance to believe. You are not the only reluctant Christian. I am one too; the more I learn, the more I realize how I fall short. But I learned one lesson well: Christianity is all about forgiveness. You may find new faith or strengthen old faith in these pages. Either way you will learn more about what Christians believe and can make up your own mind.

This book grows out of classes I taught to inquirers in Chicago in the 1960s and in Washington in the 1970s. At Chicago's St. Mary's Chapel my inquirers were mostly young men and women engaged to marry Catholics. They were uniformly starry-eyed but skeptical, determined to discover what they were getting into by marrying a practicing Christian. At St. Alban's Parish in Washington my inquirers were mostly middle-aged churchgoers who were attempting to replace childhood Sunday school training with something worthy of grown-ups. I am grateful to them all.

With the rare exception of passages I quote from other books, the information in this book cannot readily be traced to specific sources. It comes from parochial school, from years in a seminary after college, and from graduate school after that. It comes from Christians I have admired, and from the books of C. S. Lewis, Thomas Merton, Frank Sheed, and G. K. Chesterton as well as the early church fathers. There is nothing original here, nor should there be, because you want authenticity, not creativity. While this is in no sense a new version of Christianity, I hope the approach is fresh enough to keep your interest and to get you thinking. My wife, Becky, who finds religion less compelling than I, has challenged me on every page. My faith is clearer and less flabby because of her, and I am grateful.

I do plead guilty to borrowing from a script commissioned by the Paulist Press in the 1970s for what was intended to be a thirty-two installment audio-visual history of Christianity. It never was made so publisher Kevin Lynch graciously returned the rights to me.

Books are team efforts. I was blessed to have Michael Smith at Indiana University and Megan Butler and Jennifer Reist at Regnery as my editors, and Carol Huff, who typed the manuscript. I am indebted to Alfred Regnery for believing in the book.

Finally, I thank Lord Donald Coggan, 101st archbishop of Canterbury, for his blessings during my years as chairman of the College of Preachers—an institution dear to his heart and ministry. I had long since reverted to life as a preoccupied layman when I met him. Yet he encouraged me to think and minister confidently as a Christian.

David Yount
Montclair, Virginia
August, 1993

ACKNOWLEDGEMENTS

Selected prayers in Chapter 6 are taken from *The Communion of Saints: Prayers of the Famous*, edited by Horton Davies (Eerdmans, 1990); *The Oxford Book of Prayer*, edited by George Appleton (Oxford University Press, 1985); and *The Thoughts of Marcus Aurelius Antonius*, translated by John Jackson (Oxford University Press, 1934). The poem by Emily Brontë was included in *The Professor, Tales from Angria and Emma: A Fragment*, by Charlotte Brontë (Collins, 1954). Thanks to my wife who made this selection. For the brief profiles of Protestant churches in Chapter 12 I am indebted to the authors of "The Major Protestant Denominations" in the *Encyclopedia Britannica*, 15th edition, 1988. For the brief narrative on Evangelical and Pentecostal movements in the same chapter I am indebted to Harvey Cox, "Why God Didn't Die," *Nieman Reports at Harvard University*, Summer 1993. I hope the reader will be attracted to the sources, which are invariably better than anyone's commentary on them.

I fled Him, down the nights and down the days;
 I fled Him, down the arches of the years;
 I fled Him, down the Labyrinthine ways
 of my own mind; and in the mist of tears
I hid from him, and under running laughter.

—FRANCIS THOMPSON, *The Hound of Heaven*

GROWING IN FAITH

CHAPTER 1

THE RELUCTANT CHRISTIAN

The older I get the more often I encounter men and women who practice no religion but would like to believe. "I envy you your faith," they tell me. "I wish I had it, but I guess I'm just not religious."

I don't think of myself as very religious. I don't spend a lot of time in church or praying or reading the Bible. I believe, but not without grappling with doubt. I don't bring up God in casual conversation, and I am embarrassed by preachers who fancy they are in intimate contact with the Deity. Moreover, I have friends and colleagues who profess no religious faith at all but who act in a more Christian manner than I do.

My friends dismiss my protests: "You have the gift of faith," they insist. "We don't."

Nonsense. It is high time to destroy the myths that keep good people from discovering and believing in something more than themselves. Religious faith, I concede, is a gift, but it is freely given and there is plenty to go around. No one is born religious, nor is religiosity a character trait. Unless you resist it, religion is in your pores.

What is religious faith? It is not a hunger that needs to be satisfied. God-seeking is neither a passion nor a compulsion. But once someone finds him, religion gets to be a habit, one that serves a person well without becoming a preoccupation. In this respect religion is like marriage after the honeymoon—something you cherish and preserve and act on, but not obsessively.

Most American adults got a taste of religion in their childhood and many chose not to develop that taste beyond their teens. It is easy for some of them to associate religion with churchgoing, with stiff Sunday clothes, with being bored but not free to squirm, with pious and fantastic stories, and with the many sinful things one mustn't do. Many otherwise intelligent adults believe that, although they have grown up, religion has not; it remains childish. In fact, the church that seems so childish was simply trying to accommodate our own immaturity. Just as graduate school is different from kindergarten, adult religion is something else altogether from Sunday school.

This book is for the many men and women who would like to believe but don't know how or what to believe, that is, for reluctant Christians. I could have used such a book earlier in my life, but all I could find at the time were tomes of theology and diaries of "inspiration." Neither category satisfied me. I didn't want to be a religious specialist and I couldn't be convinced by sermons or sentimentality. As a young adult I wasn't prepared to discard the God of my childhood, yet I needed a grown-up faith.

What I write here is not very sophisticated, but it is adult and reliable. Don't look for controversy in these pages. Although I won't avoid dissension, I have no denominational axe to grind. I want to support the search, not carry on debate. What I want to share with the reader is simply basic Christianity, the things Christians have in common. Christianity's common ground is plenty wide for us to explore without our having to venture beyond. The reader can decide later whether the particular perspectives that Catholics or Baptists or Evangelicals offer should be owned as well.

Christianity is not just a personal conviction to be cherished in private. It is a communal faith and is tested and supported by other men and women. The church provides such a community. People who believe find a congregation that supports and tests the faith that is within them. But it is counterproductive to begin exploring Christianity by concentrating on the differences among the churches. We do well to remember that Jesus spoke only to two categories of people—Jews and pagans—not to Christians. Thus we can start confidently by considering what these people made of what he told them.

I am not going to attempt to prove the truth of Christianity to the reader, but only its plausibility. Jesus worked miracles out of compassion, not as advertisements for himself. Most of those who listened to Jesus were attracted to him by the force of his character and his message, not by his showmanship. Religious conviction in any case is not certitude; it is faith forever grappling with doubt. If Christianity could be proven without a shadow of a doubt, there would still be room for indifference.

WHY BELIEVE?

One must not think it strange to be attracted to faith. We all want to be faithful—to ourselves and to others. Christians believe that men and women are really seeking integrity—wholeness—through faith and that we cannot achieve it without the Creator who designed us and knows how we are made to work properly. Faith also offers us perspective, a place to stand and view with calm purpose and some understanding of what appears to be a bewildering and often tragic universe.

Philosophy is no substitute for religion. At best those who are only philosophical confront life's cruelties and uncertainties with dignity and responsibility, and they prevail or fail as brave victims. But those who view life through the eyes of faith see order beneath apparent chaos and hope for redemption beyond tragedy. Those who believe are enabled to view themselves and their place in life from God's perspective.

Christians believe that it is God's faith in us that allows

us to have faith in him. God grasps the initiative; we re-spond. If we seek God, it is because God has already found us and we are only waking to that fact.

Many who would like to believe are put off because Christianity is a lot to swallow and traditionally means acting out one's faith as a member of a church congregation with unfamiliar rituals. Worse, many candidates for faith are deterred because of the common equation of religion with goodness. I often hear the not-quite-honest statement "I'm not ready to believe," when the meaning is "I'm not yet ready to change my behavior and act as a Christian all the time."

This dissembling reluctance is often prompted by the rather accurate observation that a lot of churchgoing Christians don't lead exemplary lives anyway. "Aren't they just hypocrites? Should I add to their numbers?"

SIN AND VIRTUE

Our own experience tells us that vice and virtue coexist in every person. No one is all bad nor all good, nor is anyone good or bad all the time. In Robert Louis Stevenson's fiction, the good Dr. Jekyll and the evil Mr. Hyde were two distinct personalities sharing one body, but in real life good and evil are entwined. Goodness cannot be a precondition for faith; if it were no one would believe. Quite the opposite is true: faithfulness inspires us to better behavior.

There are legions of complacent Christians. Their complacency does not disprove their faith but simply reveals it to be a dormant habit.

Jesus came to love the sinner and to forgive the sin. He did not bother much with people who kept all the rules. In fact, he was inclined to condemn them for not having a heart. Do not be deterred from religion by fear that Christianity will force you to clean up your act. All of us have misgivings about our behavior and want to be better persons. Because faith gives us purpose, religion helps us to behave better and to be more aware when we fall short.

The Christian preoccupation with sin is simply an acknowledgement that we do not live up to our own expectations, let alone God's, and that we often act badly toward others by what we do or neglect to do. Sin is simply the human condition of a want of integrity—with head, heart, and behavior at odds. Sin is a kind of moral schizophrenia in which we are in conflict with ourselves first of all. This confusion is reflected in how we deal with others and with God.

Sin is the expression of a flaw characteristic of human beings. Animals, however cruel, do not sin because their behavior flows directly from design and works for their self-preservation. An animal can intimidate and kill, but only a man or woman can hate and murder. Christians believe that we inherit this flaw but that it cannot be blamed on God; it is the consequence of a primordial revolt against him. The extraordinary story of Jesus makes sense only as God's initiative to bring an end to this revolt and to mend this flaw that makes us enemies of ourselves and our fellow creatures. The single greatest impediment to faith is an unwillingness to acknowledge this flaw and to rely on God to save us from ourselves.

THE UNIQUENESS OF JESUS

After nearly two thousand years Jesus is so familiar a figure in the Western world that we forget how utterly unprecedented he was. It will not do simply to characterize him as a good and self-sacrificing man and a compelling moral teacher. There have been other teachers and other good men and women who lived longer lives of service than Jesus. Why, among all the moral heroes, does he stand out?

Jesus makes sense only if we believe what he said about himself: that he was the Son of God, sent by God to reconcile us to God. He chose sinners rather than the best people as his friends, and he praised poverty over wealth. He allowed righteous people to torture and murder him, explaining that his suffering was necessary to bring God's creatures back to God. After death he returned to life and promised his followers an eternal life of happiness.

Jesus has to be accepted or rejected by his own self-characterization and nothing less. If we counter that he was good but deluded, he is of no use to us. If we deny his Resurrection, we deny our own and are left with transient and accidental lives.

Faith is a difficult virtue because the truth about Jesus is hard to swallow and it must be swallowed without seasoning. But this is clear: Jesus believed his own story and died an ignominious death for attempting to convince others of it. His followers endured incredible hardships spreading the faith. Yet Christianity has endured for two thousand years.

A CIVILIZED FAITH

Picture a team of anthropologists coming upon a lost tribe whose members worship a loving God who had sent his son to live as one of them, teaching, healing, and forgiving them, and finally being tortured and executed so they might be saved. Imagine that this tribe was taught to live by love and forgiveness and to find virtue in poverty. Imagine that their God promised that they would never die but live eternally in happiness with him. "What a charming faith! What a civilized people!" we would exclaim. Yet this is precisely what Christians have always believed. Somehow the charm has worn thin. Why?

I believe the answer lies in the literal and minimal way we people in the Western world tend to think. Remember that Jesus was from the Orient. He spun stories rather than reciting rules and giving orders. Christianity, which thrived when transplanted to the West, gradually absorbed our Western mentality, which is fundamentally analytical. That does not make our faith wrong, of course, but it means that often we lose some of the spirit and the poetry of the faith in translation. Practical peoples tend to look at bottom lines: What is the minimum I must believe? What is the least I can get away with and still keep my membership?

On the other hand, the virtue of Western thinking protected Christianity from fuzzy thinking and rosy myths. There are things Christians cannot adequately explain, but there is nothing unclear about what they do believe. Wars have been fought, heads severed, and bodies burned at the stake in often-misguided attempts to keep Jesus' message pure. Persecution cannot be justified, but drastic measures were chosen rather than allow faith to degenerate into flabbiness or sentimentality.

It is tempting to say that it is more important how people behave than what they believe. But the long experience of Christianity suggests that people tend to behave badly whatever the circumstances. The way we act is more likely to be an expression of how we think than the other way around. A savage does not stop to justify what we (but not he) might see as his savagery, but a Christian must at least rationalize how he acts with what he professes. His awareness of the discrepancy testifies to the basic assumption that faith and life are connected. Faith does not guarantee good behavior but it mitigates our worst inclinations. For this reason it is important that faith be clear and precise.

Faith is not just the act of believing but the propositions

we believe. Just as the United States is governed not only by tradition and patriotism but also by a written constitution and laws, Christianity protects itself from shifting sentiment by clear articles of faith. If this sounds cold and legalistic consider that Christianity is essentially an insurance policy, and we know how much fine print is in the provisions.

THE PURPOSE OF LIFE

At the age of six in my first grade catechism I was taught the purpose of life. Although I was not a distinguished student of the catechism, at least I memorized these words: "The purpose of life is to know, to love, and to serve God in this world, and to be happy with him in the next."

Even as a child I found fault with that proposition. If God is self-sufficient, what can he possibly need from me? How do I love someone invisible and awesome, and how can I know him when he is literally beyond defining? As a child I did not express my skepticism in precisely those words, but I wondered. The basic proposition seemed to be a set-up: If I did things for God during my lifetime, I would be rewarded in some other time and place, but I was not told where or when or what the prize would be.

As a child, of course, I assumed the purpose of life was to know, love, and serve myself in this world and to be happy here and now. As I came to realize later, there was nothing apparently wrong with proceeding in this way; the only problem was that it did not work out. Self-knowledge is achieved by very few, and not without something extrinsic—a person, design, or faith that tells us who we are.

Self-love usually does not rise above selfishness. Spoiling oneself puts other people off and only occasionally satisfies. Despite devoting themselves to serving Number One, many persons are their own worst enemies and are bitterly disappointed in themselves. So much for the promised outcomes of self-love! As for fulfillment this side of the grave, it typically requires an abundance of health, wealth, and intellect plus the willingness of others to indulge our whims. Such favorable conditions are rare.

Let us return then, provisionally, to the purpose of life I memorized as a six year old, and see whether it isn't more credible than I thought at the time. If God wants me to know, love, and serve him in this lifetime, then it must be possible to do so. In some sense he "needs" me or at least wants my intelligent love and service. He is not promising happiness now, but only when I am close enough to him that I can't help but share his joy. Moreover, if I reflect on the life of Jesus and other Christians, as well as the misery of much of mankind, I cannot reasonably expect absolute contentment in this world, no matter how hard I may try to attain it.

GOOD GOD, EVIL WORLD

A major impediment to faith, of course, is to embark upon the task of reconciling the reality of the miseries of mankind with the reality of a good God. Perhaps this mystery holds you back: "How can I believe in a loving God who allows the suffering of innocent persons?" Facile answers to the persistence of pain are that there is no God, or (if he exists) he is uncaring or powerless.

There is no completely satisfying explanation to the problem of a good God who is powerful and sovereign over an evil world. Pain remains a paradox to even the most knowledgeable believers; nevertheless, it is not an utter mystery.

For starters, the Bible is filled with stories about the miseries of those whom God chose for his missions. God does not spare his friends, nor did he spare Jesus from torture and death. God's goodness cannot be equated with special treatment. The Bible's heroes and heroines endured worse treatment than ordinary believers. Good intentions and clean hands evidently do not ensure a pain-free life.

But that does not explain why the innocent suffer. It is one thing to choose heroism, quite another to be a victim. To help unravel this mystery we must note two things: (1) much that goes wrong in life is accidental, not intentional, and (2) much that causes pain is caused not by God but by men and women themselves. Can we blame God for the excesses of nature that engulf men, women, and children in their turmoil? Not unless we expect that God sits in a control room twenty-four hours a day pressing all of nature's buttons. And can we blame God for the murders, rapes, and wars caused by human beings? Again, unless God were to brainwash us and control us like robots, our freedom and our perversity will always allow us to commit outrageous acts of injustice, oppression, and selfishness on our fellow men and women.

It is not satisfying to acknowledge that God steps aside and allows nature (and human nature) to cause pain, but the alternative—a totally programmed world, a world without human freedom—is not desirable either. We are left with a mystery, but one in which men and women are responsible for taming the excesses of physical nature and their own natures. God offers love and salvation and a pattern of responsible living but no sure promise of good times this side of the grave.

BORN AGAIN?

Do not be deterred from your quest for faith by Christians who insist upon your being aware of having been, at a certain moment, "born again"—an experience that may have eluded you and certainly has escaped me. The born-again experience carries great emotional conviction but it is not a prerequisite to faith. Jesus requires his followers to be "born of water and the Spirit" (John 3:5), and this is accomplished in the rite of Baptism.

All Christians share the mission to preach the good news of salvation and to bring others to Jesus. Evangelism is not the exclusive prerogative of Fundamentalists or Evangelicals. And if "born again" suggests living on a high spiritual plane every moment, then let the truth be known: the everyday life of faith is not necessarily an emotional high. Religion at times can be a desert, and faith must be sustained sometimes without any emotional support whatsoever. Jesus himself briefly felt abandoned, but he persisted to his death.

The enthusiasm of some Christians can discourage the serious inquirer who seeks a faith that will weather both good and bad times. This is not to denigrate the "born again" experience but to put it in the context of a special incentive to faith. I liken it to falling in love. Many people never have that experience of total infatuation with another that we liken to "falling." But it does not preclude their loving others or believing in romantic passion, though they do not themselves feel it. Faith is not a "high" but a habit.

The enthusiasm of Evangelical Christians is not shared by all believers. Some Christians practice a quiet, almost intellectual faith. These are usually only differences of approach, not of substance. We all clothe ourselves in God, but not necessarily in the same uniform.

WHAT CHRISTIANS HAVE IN COMMON

So what is it that constitutes a Christian? <u>In simplest terms a Christian is a baptized person who responds to Jesus' invitation to repent and to follow him</u>. A Christian "convert" is one who has figuratively "turned around," abandoning a life of self-seeking in exchange for one of following Jesus and serving him. There is more to being a Christian than this, but if we look at the brief encounters of men and women with Jesus in the Gospels, this is what they all had in common, particularly the non-Jews who could not be expected to share Jesus' own rich heritage of belief as a Jew.

In apostolic times (the first generation after Jesus) whole families were converted to Jesus. That meant that every member of the family was brought into the family of God. Today many Christian churches continue to baptize infants, thus bringing them into the family of God, because faithful parents bring them to the church and dedicate themselves to raising their children in Christ's love. Babies cannot be expected to express their faith through conversion. That comes later with Confirmation. Despite differences in the practice of infant Baptism, all Christians agree that men and women must respond with faith to Jesus, and that requires a certain emotional and intellectual development. Faith is an adult virtue.

Christians believe "in" Jesus. When friends or lovers say

they believe in each other, they mean that they trust one another. Believing "in" Jesus means trusting him to keep his promises, but also two additional things. Faith means believing Jesus is who he said he is, namely the Son of God. More radically, it means believing in some way *as* Jesus believes—literally identifying our faith with his faith, so we are incorporated in his own relationship with God, so he is somehow believing for and with us. The Apostle Paul speaks often of being "in Christ," and that unity is part of what believing in Jesus means.

Am I losing you here? It will become clear eventually. Christianity is a very personal faith and it invites an intimacy with Jesus—and hence with God—that is hard to put into words (as all relationships are) but is nonetheless what religion is all about. Christianity claims that God not only created us "in his image" but that he became human himself in order to bridge even further the gap between the human and the divine. Jesus is not just a role model for us to emulate. He transports us with him in his accomplishments. What he has done, we can do because he has done it.

STAYING CONVERTED

The impulse of faith that makes one a Christian is one of conversion. But do not suppose that, once converted, a believer is magically transformed. That is simply not anyone's experience, and Christianity is a realistic religion. The life of faith is not just a matter of keeping rules. Plenty of people can claim to be law-abiding, but they are not necessarily worthy of admiration. They have simply managed to stay out of jail. Likewise, in sports following the rules of the game does not necessarily make one a good sportsman or a gracious winner or loser. In real life we judge people by their generosity and responsibility. So does God. A good person is one who can be counted on not just for the minimum but for much more.

Whereas other religions merely require their followers to follow rules and rituals, Christianity invites them to be like Jesus—totally self-giving. But Christianity is realistic enough to know that you and I will fall short, sometimes repeatedly, and for that there is always forgiveness. Of course, the availability of forgiveness in Christianity can be misconstrued as an invitation to hypocrisy, but here again Jesus warns us not to judge one another but to let God (who knows our hearts) be our judge.

Historically, we must concede that Christianity is a religion that demands much of its adherents, but we must also concede that it is a religion that acknowledges the weakness and incompleteness of its believers. Here, in portions of the fifth chapter of the Gospel According to Matthew, is but a sampling of what Jesus proclaims to be Christian being and Christian behavior:

Blessed are the poor in spirit, for theirs is the kingdom of heaven.

Blessed are those who mourn, for they shall be comforted.

Blessed are the meek, for they shall inherit the earth.

Blessed are those who hunger and thirst for righteousness, for they shall be satisfied.

Blessed are the merciful, for they shall obtain mercy.

Blessed are the pure in heart, for they shall see God.

Blessed are the peacemakers, for they shall be called sons of God.

Blessed are those who are persecuted for righteousness' sake, for theirs is the kingdom of heaven.

Blessed are you when men revile you and persecute you and utter all kinds of evil against you falsely on my account.

Let your light so shine before men, that they may see your good works and give glory to your Father who is in heaven.

You have heard that it was said, "You shall love your neighbor and hate your enemy." But I say to you, Love your enemies and pray for those who persecute you, so that you may be sons of your

Father who is in heaven; for he makes his sun rise
on the evil and on the good, and sends rain on the
just and on the unjust.

   You, therefore, must be perfect, as your
heavenly Father is perfect.

   (MATTHEW 5:3–11; 16; 43–45; 48)

The stunning climax is that Jesus expects us to be as
perfect as God himself. Rather than dismiss this out of
hand as hyperbole, consider it for what it is—an extraordinary compliment to those who love God. If we are called
to imitate God, it must be because we are already made in
his image.

WHAT CHRISTIANS BELIEVE

It took three centuries for Christians to forge a majority
agreement on what Christians believe. Here is the formulation of the Council of Nicea at an international gather-
ing of Christian leaders in 325 A.D. It is known as the
Nicene Creed:

   I believe in one God the Father Almighty, Maker of
   heaven and earth, And of all things visible and invisible: And in one Lord Jesus Christ, the only-begotten
   Son of God, Begotten of his Father before all worlds,

God of God, Light of Light, Very God of very God, Begotten, not made, Being of one substance with the Father, By whom all things were made: Who for us men and for our salvation came down from heaven, And was incarnate by the Holy Ghost of the Virgin Mary, And was made man, And was crucified also for us under Pontius Pilate. He suffered and was buried, And the third day he rose again according to the Scriptures, And ascended into heaven, And sitteth on the right hand of the Father. And he shall come again, with glory, to judge both the quick and the dead: Whose kingdom shall have no end.

And I believe in the Holy Ghost, The Lord, and Giver of Life, Who proceedeth from the Father and the Son, Who with the Father and the Son together is worshipped and glorified, Who spake by the Prophets. And I believe one holy Catholic and Apostolic Church. I acknowledge one Baptism for the remission of sins. And I look for the Resurrection of the dead. And the Life of the world to come. Amen.

Most of the wording is straightforward and clear, but in fact the Creed was composed in the wake of three centuries of violent disagreement. So each phrase—like a lawyer's brief, or a constitutional article—has a precision that only theologians can truly appreciate. The Creed not only states what Christians believe, but by implication what they should not believe; for example, that Jesus, though truly human, was not just human; and that the many communities of believers were not each unique but constituted one universal church.

Does such precision really matter? Christendom has been in much agreement on that. It does matter. But we must recognize that theological affirmation is largely deduced from what is overtly revealed and what is clearly implied in revelation. Jesus, who was raised in the legalistic tradition of first-century Judaism, elected not to express his message in legal terms but to preach by parable and example. He did not issue a creed of his own in so many words, so it had to be compiled by others from his revelation. As generations passed and the inspiration of Jesus passed into tradition, it became increasingly important to be specific. Just as the American Revolution was first initiated by and then preserved in the Declaration of Independence and, later, the American Constitution, the phenomenon of Jesus Christ, his person and his meaning for the world, is preserved in the Creed.

THE GOOD BOOK

There is a considerable temptation to treat the Bible as a kind of tangible, portable Christianity—faith in the palm of the hand. In courts and public life Americans literally take oaths with their hand resting on the Bible. Christianity is often referred to as a "religion of the book" because it has the advantage of a fixed written reference. But it is easy to overstate this advantage. The Bible comprises Christianity in the fashion that a cookbook can be said to comprise all the meals contained in its recipes. Just as a hungry man will not be satisfied with a cookbook, the Christian will not be satisfied just by reading the Bible.

To use another metaphor, a book of maps gives directions, but it does not guarantee passage. Idolatry is the enemy of all religious faith; it is tempting to idolize the Bible and appropriate it simply for one's own purposes. Even the Devil quotes the Bible for his own purposes.

The final collection of books that constitute the Bible was not established until forty-two years after the church agreed on the Christian creed. Remember that the Creed itself took three centuries to be formed, yet it antedated the canonical Bible as we know it. St. Athanasius, who authored the Nicene Creed as a young man, as an old man used his considerable personal influence to propose which books ought to be included in the New Testament. Fifteen years later Pope Damasus called a synod in Rome to accept St. Jerome's plea for the New Testament outlined by Athanasius. Jerome's Latin translation of both Old and New Testament, the Vulgate, did not appear until almost four hundred years into the Christian era but it would serve Christianity for a thousand years and inspire countless translations in vernacular languages.

The Bible as we know it comprises the books of the Old and New Testaments. The Old Testament is essentially the

Bible that Jesus himself knew. It reveals the covenant or agreement made by God with the patriarch Abraham and the Jewish people some eighteen centuries earlier. The New Testament presumes the Old but reveals a successor covenant forged through Jesus and made available to non-Jews as well. Christians believe the Bible is inspired by God, but not all of it is inspirational nor is it a "how-to" guide for the believer.

The Bible's individual books were written at different times for distinctive purposes, and the intention of the authors was not always literal or scientific. Evangelical Christians, in contrast to Catholics and mainline Protestant Christians, tend to interpret the Bible literally. However, all Christians, whatever their predilections, must do some interpreting. Fortunately there is a lot of help from modern biblical scholarship, which even non-believers agree is scientific.

THE CHURCH

The Bible is where we find the story of mankind's salvation, beginning with the story of creation in Genesis and concluding with the end of the world in the Book of Revelation. The Bible is where we meet the real-life heroes and heroines—from Noah to the apostles—who played a role in God's initiatives toward mankind.

Because there are many Christian denominations but

one Bible, it is only natural to look upon the Bible as normative—the one reference that all believers agree on. While the Bible is a norm for all kinds of Christians, one cannot diminish the importance of the church nor presume that one can be a "Bible Christian" without being a "church Christian." That is why I have taken pains to show that it was the church that defined the Bible, not the other way around.

Just as the Bible is more than a book I can hold in my hand, the church is more than a building that is mostly empty except on Sundays. The church, as opposed to individual church buildings or specific denominations, is an institution that comprises and serves all Christians. Just as marriage is an institution distinct from actual married men and women, and the American presidency is distinct from whoever happens to reside at the moment in the White House, so the church has a persistent identity and function that is not just the sum total of all individual believers. If but one man or woman remains at the end of the world, the church remains, because it is the lingering presence of Jesus.

If that sounds too mystical for you now, I will attempt to explain it later. For the present consider that key institutions have a kind of timelessness and incorruptibility about them. Marriage is not corrupted by the fact that half the unions of American men and women end in divorce. The presidency does not lose its character because one resident departs the White House in disgrace.

Just so, the church, which has suffered from the vanity, ignorance, and cruelty of many men and women who have presumed to speak for it, was not itself corrupted. The church is the agent through which God's Spirit—the Life-Giver—works. It is a conduit not only for Jesus' teaching but for God's grace and our prayers.

The church is also the flesh-and-blood expression of God's kingdom on earth. Christian love is the highest expression of faith, and love requires that people care for one another. Even Christian monks, hidden from the world, live in community, because it is only in life with one another that Christianity can be expressed.

"Wherever two or three are gathered together in my name, I am in the midst of them," Jesus promised. God is no individual's exclusive property, nor can Christianity be lived privately. God belongs to each man and woman precisely because we find him in one another. The church is God's corporate presence in the world. The reluctant Christian often finds it easy to love God but hard to love his or her fellowman and woman, but the latter is the test of the former. The epistle in the New Testament known as 1 John is a treatise on the topic and makes clear the Christian's obligation to love his or her neighbor.

THE DISADVANTAGES OF BEING
A CHRISTIAN

Every seventh day in America more than 100 million people express their Christian faith by worshiping in a church.
This statistic alone gives pause to anyone who is inclined
to dismiss out of hand a faith that is now two thousand
years old. That there are other religions that command
people's allegiance is not an argument against Christianity
but an indication of the perennial pull of faith.

Because I have dedicated this small book to the reluctant Christian, I am wary of promising more than Christianity means to deliver. It is a demanding religion, but it is
forgiving. Christianity is complex, yet the command of its
leader—"Follow me"—is simple. Its focus, Jesus, is full of
paradox, but he is as compelling today as he was in his
lifetime.

Karl Marx criticized religion as the "opiate of the
masses," numbing them from confronting the possibilities
of the present and sinking them in dreams of a future life.
In point of fact Christianity is short on consolation and
long on challenge. It is an active religion with a social
agenda that concentrates on this world. Far from relying
on magic and miracles, it depends on sacrifices, with Jesus
himself as the model, giving his life for us.

Christianity may not make your life any easier and may
actually make it harder. Nevertheless, if you abate your

reluctance and give faith a chance, you will find that your life is grounded as never before. You will have found a place to stand and a perspective that throws light on what previously may have perplexed you. You may not find your fellowman more lovable, but you will see him through God's love as equally deserving of your concern. Most important, you will begin a relationship with Jesus that will enrich your life beyond anything I can suggest, and he will be faithful to you even when you falter. St. Paul, the very first reluctant Christian, expressed it this way:

Who shall separate us from the love of Christ? . . . For I am sure that neither death, nor life, nor angels, nor principalities, nor things present, nor things to come, nor powers, nor height, nor depth, nor anything else in all creation, will be able to separate us from the love of God in Christ Jesus our Lord.

(ROMANS 8:35; 38–39)

QUESTIONS FOR DISCUSSION OR SELF-STUDY:

1. Can anyone get through life by believing only in what comes through his or her senses?

2. Are we justified in doing whatever we want so long as we don't hurt other people?

3. What is unique about Christianity that makes it different from other religious faiths?

4. What is the purpose of life?

5. If we are otherwise responsible persons, why does Christianity require our repentance and conversion?

CHAPTER 2

AWAKENING TO GOD

The world was already old when the first human opened his eyes upon the wonder of creation. Primitive man was awed, and afraid. Unlike the animals, who were equipped with natural defenses and the instinct for survival, comfortably fitted to their environment, men and women were naked, exposed to the elements, possessing neither armor nor natural weapons, nor even trustworthy instincts. They had but one weapon—their wits—to enable them to survive.

It was precisely his wits that distinguished man from his fellow creatures. But intelligence was meager consolation in a hostile environment when there was such a small fund of information and wisdom. It would take countless millennia before primitive man learned to shape his environment and to assert his domination over nature. At the outset, human reason only sharpened his awareness of pain and his anticipation of danger. Man's unique powers of imagination and anticipation would eventually free him from the limitations of his own senses, his own time and place. But initially imagination possessed the quality of nightmare. When danger was not physically present, it was present in anxious anticipation—in man's mind. Even when primitive man was warm and his belly full, he could imagine the inevitable pangs of hunger and the coming of winter.

THE PRIMITIVE IMAGINATION

Early expressions of the primitive imagination can be seen in the cave drawings in Spain. They are artistic even by modern standards, but they were not meant to be decorative. The primitive artists, in depicting the hunt, were rehearsing for the inevitable combat, the need to kill to survive.

Modern man, by contrast, subdues nature through technology. By unlocking nature's laws we now manipulate creation, bending it to our own uses. Rather than submit to the environment on its own terms, we create artificial environments to suit ourselves. Primitive man was no less determined to control nature. He did it through magic. Spells, incantations, elaborate formulas, and arcane rites were devised to summon food for the hungry, rain for the thirsty earth, sun against the cold, health for the sickly, and fertility for the barren.

Today we are inclined to regard magic as an illustration of man's gullibility. But primitive man was no fool. Alongside his practice of magic (and often indistinguishable from it), he developed a rudimentary practical science. Long before there was literature, there was scientific agriculture. Man devised magic, not to fool himself, but to trick nature. Magic was an expression of man's certitude that he was nature's superior—that by his wits he could cajole nature to serve him.

Did magic work? It certainly appeared to, but it must be remembered that primitive mankind's expectations of success were modest. Clever magicians knew enough of nature's ways to predict when rain might relieve a drought, timing their rites accordingly. Magic was a kind of vanity; however long it took for nature to reward man with food or health or warmth, primitive man took credit for making it happen.

Magic came into disrepute, not because it was ineffective, but because it became identified as an abuse of nature. As man formed communities of mutual aid, magic was regarded as too selfish, too manipulative to serve the common needs. And it was too easily converted into a weapon against other individuals: black magic. Man learned that community was the key to survival and he became willing to subordinate personal gratification to the common good. In place of fear came a respect for nature and for his comrades. In place of awe a sense of the sacred came to dominate man in his dealings with nature and with the tribe. At this point early man overcame his isolation, recognizing the spirit that animated other men and the spirits that stood behind the activity of nature. With the discernment of spirit and the sense of sacredness, religion was born.

PAGANISM

Although it was not religion as we know it, all the basic elements of religion were present in paganism:

—the sense that one must deal with the powers behind nature
—the respect for creation and recognition of the spirit in one's fellowman
—the need for shared beliefs and a consecration of the community.

Paganism is now popularly thought of as nonbelief, but it is more accurately a religion based on nature. Religion became the glue that held together the community's approach to life and expressed its values. Respect took the place of selfish manipulation. Prayer, ritual, and sacrifice were rudimentary attempts to communicate with the spirits within nature, gaining their benevolence. While even primitive man felt superior to nature, he felt inferior to the spirits, but bold enough to communicate with them.

Man and the spirits of nature had this in common: consciousness and the power of purpose. The forces he felt around himself were akin to the powers he felt within himself. In dealing with the spirits, the early human community attempted to appropriate some of their power—to share in their creative power.

It was only a matter of time until man began to personify the invisible powers, perceiving that the spirits were beings, more powerful assuredly, but not unlike himself. As the sense of the sacred developed, spirits became more generalized. Instead of a spirit for each thing and each place, a spirit was conceived as being behind related things:

—a spirit for the earth
—a spirit for the waters
—a spirit that moved the sun and stars.

In short, the spirits took on the characteristics of persons. They became gods. In Egypt, Ra was a sun god. The sky, in Greece, was personified as Zeus. In India, Ushas was conceived as god of the dawn. Gods were thought to motivate not only nature but the activities of mankind. War and agriculture had their gods, so also did the family.

THE GODS

Perhaps the most enduring god was Apollo. Through the centuries he was conceived variously as lord of the herds, master of prophecy, god of health and poetry, and finally sun-god. Even after Emperor Constantine in the fourth century became a Christian, he retained Apollo as his personal patron, depicting himself on Roman coins with the sun as his halo.

When migratory peoples began to build permanent homes for themselves, it was a logical next step to provide a home for their gods. So temples were constructed. The wizard and magician slowly gave way to the holy man and priest, that special representative of the community who offered prayer and sacrifice on behalf of his people. Prayer, initially an attempt to cast spells, slowly evolved into the outpouring of the soul to the divine. Sacrifice, begun as a crude attempt to bargain with the gods, eventually became the ritual acknowledgement that life was the gift of the spirits. Sin, initially conceived as a violation of taboo and failure to follow ritual, changed more slowly in meaning. As the gods began to be thought of not only as powerful, but also good, sin became an offense against that goodness.

As long as man was obsessed with his immediate physical needs, religion was no more than an elaborate way of fulfilling those needs. But as man joined in a society and those most pressing demands were satisfied, he discovered other needs:

—love, friendship, and respect
—truth, goodness, and beauty.

But even in the midst of community life, each man was aware of his ultimate isolation, of being the prisoner of his own body and mind, destined for a brief sojourn, then extinction. Religion, therefore, took yet a new turn, evolving into an expression of man's search for meaning: not the meaning of the world alone, but the meaning of himself.

GODS OF SILENCE

Here mankind encountered the ultimate obstacle. The gods he knew were the creatures of his own imagination. He could pray to them, ply them with sacrifices, and hope for their favor. But they did not talk to him. They kept their silence in their world of the spirit while he was held fast as prisoner in his own mortal flesh. The history of religion to this point was the chronicle of man's overtures to his gods. What remained was for the gods to respond in kind. So far, there was silence.

Two millennia before the birth of Christ, the silence was broken. Unbidden, a message came from God. He spoke to Abraham, a nomad, directing him to travel to the land between the Mediterranean Sea and the Jordan River, there to dominate the land and to father a people that would inherit the earth. The voice identified himself as the god Yahweh—"I am who am"—the god of Abraham and his descendants. Yahweh made an agreement with Abraham that would persist through every generation. The message was simple:

> I am your god;
> you are my people.
> If you will be faithful to me,
> I will be faithful to you.

From this moment, religion was no longer simply the expression of man's fear and yearning, but the relationship of God and man. God had entered history and had summoned mankind to enter into a covenant. There was no longer need to find God. God had found man.

THE COVENANT

Mankind's persistent quest for God can be regarded only as a qualified failure. It led him to the worship of nature, to the worship of idols in the form of beasts, and to the worship of political leaders and demigods who, unfortunately, shared man's faults as well as his strengths. The creature could not conceive of his Creator.

Then, unexpectedly, God revealed himself, and the character of religion was changed for all time. No longer the quest of man for his God, it became God's quest for his people and the adventure of God with man. The voice of God came to Abraham in the city of Ur near the Persian Gulf some two thousand years before Christ. In Ur there was already speculation about the possibility of but one god to account for creation. This new monotheism competed with crass idolatry and wholesale human sacrifice in the ancient Middle East.

When God announced himself to Abraham as Yahweh, the one true God, the patriarch-to-be was separated from his kindred, who remained pagans. For the rest of his life Abraham wandered in the land between the Mediterranean and the Jordan, preaching his faith, finally dying in exile as the founder of a new people, chosen to carry God's message to mankind. The message was much more than the mere revelation of God's identity. It was a partnership, or covenant, offered by God to man, to govern man's relationship with God for all time.

When Abraham was ninety-nine years old, the Lord said to him: "I am God Almighty; walk before me, and be blameless. And I will make my covenant between me and you, and will multiply you exceedingly" (Genesis 17:1–2). Abraham fell on his face in awe as God continued: "And I will establish my covenant between me and you and your descendants after you throughout their generations for an everlasting covenant, to be God to you and to your descendants" (Genesis 17:7).

TESTS FOR FAITHFULNESS

The price of being thus chosen was constantly to be tested for faithfulness. Abraham himself was tested, whether he loved God more than his own son, who was his most precious gift from God. When he was told to sacrifice his son, Isaac, Abraham was restrained by God only at the last moment of trial.

Famine forced Abraham's progeny into Egypt where they were enslaved but maintained a kernel of faith in their one God. Then, thirteen or fourteen centuries before Christ, one of them, Moses, led his people out of Egypt for a lifetime of wandering in the Sinai desert before reentering Canaan as their Promised Land. In the desert, the Chosen People found even harsher challenges than slavery under the pharaohs. But here in the blistering sun and the blowing sands there were no distractions from God, who led them onward even as he tested them.

God's people became known as the Jews, taking their name from Abraham's great-grandson, Judah. God was careful to explain that he chose the Jews not because they were superior to other peoples but rather because he meant to use them in a magnificent plan of salvation for mankind.

TERMS OF THE COVENANT

What did the covenant require? Man must serve God by imitating God's ways: As he is just and merciful, so you must be just and merciful. The great commandment was this: You shall love the Lord your God with all your heart, with all your might, and with all your soul. The covenant was sealed through the sign of circumcision. Every Jewish male was to bear this mark, associated with the powers of life-giving, and a reminder of the suffering to be undergone in a life of faithfulness.

Moses brought from God the familiar Ten Commandments, which we have come to recognize as basic to civilized life but which were radical in that time of cruelty and infidelity. Yahweh proclaimed himself to be the one God and forbade idolatry. He commanded that one day in every seven be set aside from life's business as a day of rest, meditation, and prayer. He commanded respect for parents—for mother as well as father at a time when women were denigrated. Murder, theft, lying, and adultery were violations of the covenant. So, too, was envy of one's fellowman and of his possessions. A harsh justice was allowed but not in the spirit of revenge. Criminals were to be treated in the measure of their crimes. "An eye for an eye; tooth for tooth" was a considerable advance in civilization for a people who tortured and murdered for slight offenses.

The covenant imposed a disciplined life. Over the centuries, the basic law delivered by Moses was extended to include prescriptions for faithful behavior in matters of hygiene, inheritance, property, agriculture, diet, and the conduct of business. Life's smallest details became rituals of fidelity to God.

A DEMANDING GOD

Yahweh originally appeared to be an angry God, literally the god of thunder; but in time the Jews learned that he was loving in his demands. Moreover, although he had chosen them especially, he made it clear that he was God of all mankind.

The story of creation related by Moses to the Jews was unique in the ancient world because it portrayed an all-powerful God. Both Creator and his creation were good. God was neither responsible for evil nor powerless before it. He simply allowed it to exist. Moses revealed that the man and the woman, Adam and Eve, had brought evil into the world by presuming that they could judge good and evil on their own. Alone among God's creatures, men and women had freedom to reject God in favor of themselves or of other idols.

Within two centuries of their return from exile in Egypt, the Jews reached the pinnacle of their power under Kings Saul, David, and Solomon. A temple was built in Jerusalem and, for a time, it appeared that God's people would keep faith with him. But backsliding proved inevitable. The Jews lived in two adjacent kingdoms, Israel and Judah, at the very crossroads of the ancient world, where their faith in the one God was on display. They could either influence the world for good or be seduced by it. In fact, their high age of faithfulness lasted but a few generations. Even the great kings had lapsed into sin and had been punished. It was clear that no one, no matter how lofty, could escape God's demand to be faithful to his covenant.

Because they were tiny buffer states between great empires, the Jewish nations were constantly on the defensive. Wracked by internal dissent, the northern kingdom of Israel fell to Assyria toward the close of the eighth century B.C., never to recover its sovereignty. Two centuries later, at the beginning of the sixth century, Judah was overwhelmed by Babylon. The temple was destroyed and Judah's leading citizens were forced into exile. But God followed them in their hearts. Because the exiles kept faith, they were allowed to return some fifty years later. Immediately they set about rebuilding the temple.

THE AGE OF PROPHETS

But the religious leadership of the Jewish kings was never restored. Their place was taken by prophets, who traversed the land reminding the people of the covenant they had transgressed and demonstrating how conquest and exile were God's reminders of their infidelity. Three great prophets were contemporary with the Babylonian captivity: Ezekiel, Jeremiah, and Isaiah. The restoration of Judah was brilliant but brief. The nation remained a Persian dependency; a century later, there followed yet another, smaller exile. Then in 332 Judah succumbed to Alexander the Great and in turn to Egypt a dozen years later. In the year 198 B.C., Syria was the conqueror. However, thirty years later, when the Syrian king, Antiochus Epiphanes, closed the temple to worshipers, a patriotic Jewish family, the Maccabees, led a successful revolt and three years thereafter the temple was opened.

But the victory was short-lived. Sixty-three years before Christ the Roman general, Pompey, captured Jerusalem slaughtering over twelve thousand Jews and incorporating Judah into the Roman Empire.

Why such suffering for God's chosen people? The prophet Isaiah was thought to provide a clue by his reference to a "suffering servant." Although Christians would identify the servant with Jesus, many Jews came to believe it described the entire nation, destined to bear not only its own sins, but the sins of the entire world as the cost of adoption by God. The Book of Job concluded that man cannot penetrate God's ways, nor ever blame him. Suffering, whatever its justification, is a test of faith. The faithful believer does best to cry out, in the words of a poignant Hasidic prayer: "God, do not tell me why I suffer, for I am no doubt unworthy to know why, but help me to believe that I suffer for your sake!"

As subjugation and exile appeared to be the destiny of the Chosen People, the Jews found a new source of hope, intimated by the prophets. They began to look for a savior, a messiah who would restore the ancient kingdom of David and gather God's children into a reign of peace and justice. The messiah was expected to be a spiritual leader, but also a victorious political and military personage. While this glorious messiah was expected by some of the Jews, other Jews spiritualized their expectations, establishing communities of prayer and sacrifice. The Dead Sea scrolls, discovered in our own time, describe such a desert community devoted to repentance and harsh discipline to demonstrate their faithfulness and expectation. They dramatized the intertestamental world that produced the extraordinary figure of John the Baptist—a man, clothed in rags, living a life of severity in the desert, calling upon God's chosen to repent, washing them in the waters of the River Jordan as a sign of their change of heart.

John, Jesus' cousin, was the last of the prophets. Unlike his forebears, John lived to see his prophecy fulfilled. For, one day, he baptized a man who was no sinner but who would burden himself with the sins of all mankind. With the appearance of Jesus, the old covenant was superseded by a radical new agreement sealed by God's own Son, who would give his life to make it work.

ONE GOD

The Jews' discovery that there is only one God qualifies as the greatest single advance in the religious development of mankind: "Listen, Israel, our God is one God!" By insisting on but one God, the Jews could argue that the universe was conceived, created, maintained, and moved for a single purpose—for good. To believe in one God, moreover, eliminates irresponsibility toward the world. The soap opera conflicts of pagan demigods and spirits can no longer be employed to explain events. Nor can a world ruled by a single God allow evil to claim to be the equal of good, nor chance and fortune to be the mistresses of men.

If there is one God, then—undistracted and unchallenged—he cares for his creation. When man suffers evil, it cannot be blamed on God but on disruptions within creation, including man's own perversity. The Jews held to this sane belief in one God almost alone among the peoples of the ancient world. It was only natural, then, that when Jesus appeared, he seemed to threaten this cornerstone of their faith. For Jesus not only referred to himself as the unique Son of God; he claimed identity with God: "The Father and I are one," Jesus said. "He who sees me sees the Father."

THE TRINITY

When Jesus rose from the dead, it was accepted by his followers as God's own proof of his Son's divinity. The one God of Judaism now became Father and Son in Christianity. To further complicate the faith in one God, Jesus sent God's Holy Spirit to strengthen the church. He made it clear that this Spirit was also God. Almost overnight the Creator, still one and identified with the God of the Jews, was now somehow three: Father, Son, and Spirit.

Remarkably, the church has never been embarrassed by this paradox of God as one, yet three. It has treated Father, Son, and Spirit—the Trinity—not as an embarrassment, but as an enrichment of our knowledge of who God is. And why not? The God of the Jews had often seemed austere and distant—alone in his power and righteousness. Jesus proved that God was loving and caring—a God who would send his own Son to die for mankind and his Spirit to make every man and woman a son and a daughter of God.

In the Trinity God shows himself to be anything but isolated, remote, unreachable. He is vulnerable as only a lover can be vulnerable. The living God is a loving God, willing to become one of his creatures and die for them. The trinitarian God is no less Godly for caring and acting; he is more so because he is clearly not complacent but always acting on behalf of his creation. What is more, the

God of Christianity has an inner life of his own. He not only loves his creation, he is love himself: Father and Son locked in the Spirit of Love.

GOD'S INNER LIFE

This inner richness and love in God expands into creation and explains it; love, as we know, by its nature is expansive and creative. Of course, God has no need of his creatures. He is self-sufficient. But because love is God's activity within himself, creation is love's effect, patterned after the Father's love for the Son:

> In the beginning was the Word, and the Word was with God, and the Word was God. He was in the beginning with God; all things were made through him, and without him was not anything made that was made.
>
> (JOHN 1:1–3)

John is referring to Jesus when he speaks of the Word. In sharp distinction with the other Gospels (which begin their story with Jesus' forebears, his birth in Bethlehem, or his baptism by the Jordan), St. John writes that the Son of God existed from the beginning, or rather, from eternity. For St. John, Jesus is the Word or perfect expression of God, cast as the perfect model for all creation.

Jesus had said of himself, "Before Abraham was, I am," referring to the Father of the Jewish people who had lived twenty centuries earlier. Jesus' claim to a preexistence confounded his followers during his lifetime, but after the Resurrection a possibility occurred to his followers: if Jesus could live again after his death, could he not have lived before his birth?

If Jesus had a preexistence, they reasoned, it could not have been precisely as the man they had known who was born of Mary in Bethlehem in the reign of Caesar Augustus, but as Son of God not yet incarnate.

ATTEMPTS TO AVOID THE PROBLEM

A few Christian commentators have avoided the problem of the Son's preexistence altogether by maintaining that Jesus the man had been somehow chosen or enhanced or divinized at the moment of his baptism. But this does not square with Jesus' own claim to a prior existence with God.

In the second century the mystical heresy known as Gnosticism took the opposite tack in defining the nature of Jesus. Gnostics, contending that everything physical is evil, concluded that Jesus could not have been anything but a phantom man: he was God pretending or seeming to be a human being (a view generally known as docetism).

The Arian heresy, which attracted more Christians in the late fourth century than the traditional Church, came back the other way by insisting that Jesus, though extraordinary, was but a creature like the rest of us with a beginning in time. In their defense, Arians cited St. Paul's letter to the Colossians, which related that Christ was "the first-born of all creation," interpreting this to mean that Jesus had a beginning in creation, unlike God the eternal Creator. Moreover they cited the great church father, Tertullian, who also reasoned that the Son of God had a beginning in time, not eternity. Traditional Christians took as their authority the prologue to St. John's Gospel and the Eastern Church father, Origen, who insisted that Christ's beginning was timeless.

Since Scripture and church tradition offered no clear resolution, the church had to consult itself for a consensus. This it did in the first ecumenical (or worldwide) council of church leaders which met in the year 325 at Nicea. The council rejected any subordination of God the Son to God the Father. Father and Son alike were described as two "persons" sharing in one "substance." Together with the Holy Spirit, they constituted the Trinity—the three-in-one God. Look again at the creed in the previous chapter to see the formulation that they gave to the church.

THE RICHNESS OF THE TRIUNE GOD

Church leaders at Nicea revealed a rich, if paradoxical, concept. The doctrine of the Trinity assigns God both unity and plurality. He is one and he is three. As the source and foundation of all that is, God is changeless in himself. Yet in God is an eternal initiative to generate: God the Son is begotten; God the Holy Spirit proceeds from this loving relationship. The eternal three-in-one God is neither limited by time, nor is he oblivious to time, since he enters the world of his creation. Throughout Israel's history, eternity had penetrated time, as God dealt directly with humankind. In the Incarnation, God the Son entered history in person as Jesus, who is as truly human as he is divine.

The god of the philosophers could be defined only by negation: by his lack of limitations. The philosophers' god possessed neither personality nor concern for creatures. The Trinity, by contrast, is a demonstration that God has both an inner life and an external life. The God of Moses speaks and acts. As Christ, the godhead joins his creation as a man, suffering and dying to reconcile man with God. If the doctrine of the Trinity remains ultimately paradoxical, it is nevertheless the only way to account for Jesus being God and the Holy Spirit being God. Far from denying monotheism, the notion of the Trinity becomes an enhancement of the Jewish faith in one God.

The church's insistence on the Trinity against the one-God simplifiers dramatizes the difference between orthodoxy and heresy: orthodoxy unifies; heresy divides. Orthodoxy tolerates complexity and ambiguity; heresy oversimplifies and rejects what it cannot understand. Orthodoxy sees things whole; heresy separates. The act of faith is simple, but the object of faith is rich and complex.

Recall that the Gnostics had separated body and spirit. Arians separated creature from creator. In the fifth century another heretical group, the Nestorians, would attempt to explain Jesus as God and man by claiming he had two natures—in effect making Christ a split personality.

MORE ATTEMPTS TO
SIMPLIFY GOD

Nestorius became archbishop of Constantinople in 438. He refused to consider Mary the mother of God because it offended his notion of divinity to think of God as an infant at the breast. While infant dependency was permissible for Jesus the man, Nestorius argued, it was not proper for the Son of God. Eutyches, a monk of Constantinople, recognized the error of Nestorianism, but "saved" Jesus' unity as a person by denying that Christ had a human nature. Eutyches' view became the Monophysite heresy, which along with Nestorianism was repudiated by a new church council in 451. There church leaders affirmed that Jesus was at once truly human and truly divine: a single person of one substance with the Father in his divinity, and of one substance with man in his humanity.

Revisionism did not end there; it became more refined. Monothelites attempted to explain the human and divine in Jesus as a matter of two distinct wills. Joachim of Flore accused the church of preaching a fourfold God: the three persons plus the godhead!

But the battle over the three-in-one was over and the orthodox formulation of the Trinity was established. On but one matter there remained a difference within the church that continues to our day: whether the Holy Spirit proceeds from the Father and Son or from the Father alone. The latter position is taken by the Orthodox Christian churches of the East. It has never been considered critical enough to be deemed heretical and is too esoteric to concern you and me.

ATTEMPTS TO KNOW MORE ABOUT GOD

If the Trinity is ultimately beyond understanding, Christians have nevertheless attempted to see through the mist. St. Thomas Aquinas in the high Middle Ages reasoned that each of the divine persons is "as great as the whole Trinity" since "greatness signifies perfection of nature. . . . The essence and dignity of the Father and the Son is the same, but in the Father according to the relation of Giver, in the Son according to the relation of Receiver."

Earlier writers had used more vivid metaphors, comparing the relation of Father to Son as flame to its light, as spring to its stream, and as seal to its impress. "Think," said St. Augustine, "of fire as a father and light as a son . . . and it is easy to see which begets which." Contemporary Christian thinking looks to the Trinity as the foundation of our faith that God is love. Experience shows that love joins. Father, Son, and Holy Spirit—one God in the perfect love of unity. But God does not confine love within the Trinity. Each person has a role: The Father expresses God's love in creating; the Son expresses God's love in redeeming; and the Holy Spirit expresses God's love in maintaining us for an eternity. Moreover, the Trinity helps to explain Christ's founding of a church as a community of Christians. The godhead itself is a community of persons. The church is the community of human persons whom God has chosen.

Ultimately, the mystery of the Trinity is the mystery of love. In loving one gives all of oneself, yet becomes more than what one was before. The lover empties himself but is filled to overflowing. God does not turn in on himself complacently because his inner life is an eternal love affair of Father, Son, and Spirit. God's love for his creation reflects what he is: love itself.

QUESTIONS FOR DISCUSSION OR SELF-STUDY:

1. Is God a Christian?

2. Why does God test us?

3. Can God be angry and loving at the same time?

4. What was God's covenant?

5. Is the Trinity a contradiction to our faith in one God?

CHAPTER 3

JESUS AND HIS MESSAGE

He was the son of an obscure carpenter from a provincial village in a tiny defeated nation. At the age of thirty he began a brief public life. He wrote nothing that has survived, held no office, spoke from no public platform. He never left his homeland. No one bothered to note his appearance for posterity. He spoke to no more than a few thousand persons, most of them ordinary countrymen. Within three years he was dead, executed as a common criminal.

Today, nearly two thousand years later, almost 2 billion living persons are this man's followers. The world's law, literature, and standards of decency—indeed all of man's dealings with his fellowman—reflect the continuing influence of Jesus of Nazareth. The world in which we live literally reckons time from the year of his birth. It is as if time itself began coincidental with Jesus.

THE PERSISTENCE OF JESUS

Nor has Jesus' influence ever waned through the years. He was not a forgotten genius to be rediscovered by later ages; in fact, he was never "discovered" initially, but presented himself clearly and forcefully with the explicit intention of winning followers. To understand Jesus we must account for the faith of his adherents. Within a few weeks of his execution as a criminal, Jesus' principal followers, who had scattered to protect themselves, reunited in Jerusalem. There were probably no more than 120 of them, united in a common devotion to his memory, but, more importantly, by the conviction that he was alive and had been seen by some among their number. Moreover, they believed Jesus would return—and hoped it would be in their lifetimes—to save the world and bring it into a glorious eternity. The immediate personal faith of these few Christians controls what we know of Jesus because they reflected it in the Gospels—four roughly parallel accounts of his life and teaching. These accounts, written by believers for believers, follow the rules of neither history nor biography. Nor do they attempt to convince the unbelieving. Rather, they are straightforward accounts of the principal things Jesus said, did, and promised.

It is impossible to write a biography of Christ worthy of its title or subject. The Gospels account for no more than fifty days in his adult life. Nevertheless, they clearly convey his message and significance. The four gospels form the basis of a New Testament, the fulfillment of an Old Testament relating centuries of God's revelation to his chosen people, the Jews.

JESUS THE JEW

Jesus was a Jew. He spoke to the Jews in terms they uniquely understood, of the one good God, creator of the universe, who chose Israel as the object of his love and sealed an agreement or covenant requiring their faithfulness. The biblical history of the Jews as a chosen people dramatized mankind's perverse infidelity to its creator—its inability to cleave to the covenant. In the Gospels the adult Jesus makes his first appearance at the River Jordan where he submits to baptism by his cousin John. The ritual of washing was understood to signify repentance, but it was clear to John that Jesus was without sin. Only much later does it become clear that Jesus will personally assume the sins of all other men. John the Baptist yields the way to Jesus and sends his own followers after him, but not before he acknowledges Jesus as the "lamb of God," signifying Jesus' sacrificial role. As an intimation of Jesus' character, the Spirit is seen descending upon him during the baptism.

Having made this initial public appearance, Jesus retreats alone into the desert to test his resolve and to be tested by the spirit of evil. For forty days and nights he agonizes over his destiny, tempted to display his power rather than pursue his life of sacrifice. Jesus' antagonists, the Jewish religious leaders, would later demand signs of power—not the miracles that fed the hungry and cured the sick, but some great messianic act of power. In the desert the evil spirit asks Jesus to cast himself from the temple; the Jewish leaders would demand that he come down from the cross before they would believe.

DOING GOOD

"He went about doing good," the Gospels relate; but Jesus refused to make a spectacle of his power. Instead he spoke clearly and forcefully in terms even a child could understand and act upon. Although Jesus taught from the perspective of Jewish history and tradition, his thoughts were emphatically his own. The violent reactions he aroused dramatize how revolutionary were his claims.

Jesus did not speculate or philosophize. He taught, explained, described, and insisted with total authority. For Jesus, God's presence and fatherly love, his righteousness, mercy, and goodness, were not just options, but compelling facts of experience. Communion with God was, for Jesus, a conscious, accessible reality for all mankind. A Jew speaking to fellow Jews, he addressed the common experience of mankind everywhere and at all times.

Jesus' adult life, though presented only episodically in

the Gospels, falls into three stages: the first mainly in Galilee where he grew up; the second in Peraea or Samaria; and the final period in and around Jerusalem. "Jesus came into Galilee proclaiming the good news of God, that the time is fulfilled and the kingdom of God has drawn near."

Like John the Baptist before him, Jesus called for repentance, but on his lips it was a joyous call for a change of heart, mind, and life that would open mankind to adoption as sons of God. Using Capharnum as a base, he taught in synagogues, in private homes, on the slopes of hills, and by the shores of the lake. He worked wonders out of compassion for the people and to draw attention to his message, but principally to glorify God.

FAITH THE KEY

Although he worked cures for love of the afflicted, Jesus routinely required faith as the condition of performing miracles. Faith made it possible for him to show the power of God's love. As he taught and healed, Jesus made himself accessible to everyone: to the sick, the despised, the sinful; to rich and poor alike; to men, women, and children; to Jew and Gentile. He played no favorites. For him, every person was special. From among his constant companions, he chose twelve men to join his mission, to preach in his name and cure the sick. These were the apostles, men of no particular intellect, character, or standing when they were chosen, but who became great by reason of their utter attachment to Jesus.

Initially, a wave of enthusiasm greeted Jesus' ministry in Galilee, sufficient to alarm religious authorities. Jewish leaders were concerned by Jesus' independence and self-assurance. In calling for a change of heart, Jesus denigrated the complex rituals of Jewish life that had substituted robot-like observance for faithful obedience and love. As Jesus confounded his critics, revealing their hypocrisy, they came to hate and fear his success. But, by the end of the Galilean ministry, Jesus openly acknowledged that the popular enthusiasm he had enjoyed was undependable. Even his neighbors in his own childhood home of Nazareth rejected his teaching.

Jesus dramatized the rejection in a parable—a simple story with a moral—when he spoke of the farmer who planted good seed only to see it wither for want of fertile soil. Significantly, at the time of this initial rejection, Jesus chose to heal the daughter of a Gentile mother, revealing that God's concern was not restricted to the Jews alone.

THE KINGDOM

In his preaching Jesus announced a kingdom, a loving society of God's people, faithful to him and concerned for one another. In this kingdom God reigned supreme in the hearts of his people. The kingdom would be perfected in time but it was available at any time people gathered in God's name. Where two or three are gathered together in my name, Jesus promised, I will be there with you.

Jesus taught that every man, woman, and child was precious and perfectible. "Be perfect as your heavenly Father is perfect," he counseled. Appealing to the best in man, he asked, "What does it profit a man if he gain the whole world and lose his own soul?" As for sin, Jesus explained that it was something deeper than a failure to observe rituals. "What comes out of a person" defiles him, he said. The worst sin of all (the "sin against the Holy Spirit") is moral insensibility, man's rejection of mercy and love.

Jesus welcomed sinners because so many of their faults were only weaknesses. The righteous were worse because they were "hard of heart," when it was precisely a change of heart that opened mankind to receive the kingdom. Although he taught that God was a father to all who accept adoption, it was clear that Jesus was uniquely God's Son. "He who has seen me has seen the Father," he said. To know the Father is man's highest fulfillment, and the way to know him is in and through Jesus, God's only Son.

THE LAW OF LOVE

Unlike the law given by Moses, the teachings of Jesus are not embodied in a code of commandments and prohibitions. Rather than impose many strictures, Jesus gave but one law: to love. Love was not only the way to fulfillment but was fulfillment itself. Love was to bind man in his dealings with God and man alike. According to Jesus, worldly success is no indication of God's favor. Poverty and humility are not to be despised because simplicity helps to make a person wholehearted in loving service.

Jesus gradually revealed himself to his apostles. Challenged by Jesus, the Apostle Peter acknowledged that Jesus was the Messiah longed-for by the Jews. Later, at his trial, Jesus would acknowledge as much and more: that he was the Son of God. To be the Messiah was to play the role of Savior and King; but to be Son of God was to claim a unique affinity to the Father: "The Father and I are one," Jesus said. "Who sees me sees the Father."

Jesus, however, never advertised himself in these terms, preferring to call himself the "Son of Man," a mysterious reference from the prophet Daniel that emphasized Jesus' identity with mankind. Because Jesus was Son of Man, he could offer himself for mankind; because he was the Son of God, he could make a sacrifice of himself worthy of God.

THE END AND THE BEGINNING

Approaching Jerusalem at the time of the great feast of Passover, Jesus put himself into the hands of his enemies and was betrayed for thirty silver coins by one of his closest friends, the Apostle Judas. Sharing a final supper with the twelve, Jesus took bread and wine as signs of his coming sacrifice and shared with his friends as a memorial. These, he said, are my body and blood.

The next day Jesus was dead, the Jewish leaders having convinced the Roman governor that he was a threat to public order. After the Roman fashion with common criminals, Jesus was tortured and then made to carry a cross of execution, to which he was nailed hand and foot to suffer slowly until he expired. From the cross, Jesus forgave his persecutors—"they know not what they do"—and, as he breathed his last, exclaimed of his life: "It is consummated."

Consummated it was, but it was not over. The story of Jesus is neither tragedy nor melodrama. Within two days he was alive again, appearing no longer to the crowds but to his friends to whom he gave the mission of carrying his message and God's love to all mankind. When Jesus finally returned to the Father, he promised to leave God's Spirit to guide the family of believers who became his church. In conquering death, Jesus made good his promise that all who believe shall live.

A MAN OF MYSTERY

Whether or not he is acknowledged to be Son of God, Jesus of Nazareth is clearly the most influential man in history. Of what he said and did we have a sparse but adequate record. But his personality and character remain veiled. The authors of the Gospels—who knew him well—fail to tell us whether he was short or tall, dark or light, thin or heavy, quick or slow, humorous or somber. Nor did Jesus leave a letter of memoir that might offer a clue to his personality.

"Learn of me," he told those who would follow him. But succeeding generations of Christians have attempted to be Christ-like with only glimmerings of what he was like as a person, taken from what he said and did. If the Jesus we know remains a shadowy personality, it is surely intentional. Christianity has never developed as a cult of personality. Hero-worship is not to be confused with the true worship of God.

THE TEMPTATION TO REINVENT GOD

The very lack of physical detail about Jesus is an invitation for each age to reinvent him in its own image. The artistic image we have of him at the moment is a romantic one dating from the nineteenth century—bearded, tall, handsome, slightly melancholy, and Semitic. In the earliest centuries, Jesus was depicted as clean-shaven. In Constantinople, he appeared almost Oriental. African churches depict him as a black man.

Hollywood has continued the revisionism. In the film *King of Kings*, Jesus had shaven armpits like a woman.

Someone on the set apparently felt it was unseemly to depict a hairy Messiah. In the communist-inspired Italian film, *Gospel According to St. Matthew*, Jesus was a brooding, unwashed revolutionary. In *The Last Temptation of Christ*, he was a tortured dreamer. *Jesus Christ Superstar* made him a child of the 1960s. In the face of all this foolishness the Academy Award-winning *Ben Hur* adroitly avoided depicting Jesus at all. He is in the cast but always off-screen. We see his effect on others, but we do not see him.

The attempt to reinvent Jesus to make him relevant occasionally flies in the face of facts we have about him. At the 1992 Democratic National Convention, the Rev. Jesse Jackson used Jesus to promote his social agenda. "Even as we spurn the homeless on the street," Jackson urged, "remember, Jesus was born to a homeless couple, outdoors . . . He was the child of a single mother." This is simply wrong. Mary and Joseph clearly had a home in Nazareth, where Joseph was an employed carpenter. The couple was legally espoused. Jesus' conception (presuming that God was his father) was surely legitimate. True, the couple was traveling when Mary gave birth, and all hotels were full, but even the stable which became Jesus' birthplace offered more comfort and privacy than a ghetto street in a modern American city.

Fortunately, the Gospels tell us enough about Jesus to make it unnecessary to cosmeticize him for each new generation. The Gospel accounts are remarkably straightforward. The Jesus we meet there is not quaint but direct. He does not need to be more "modern."

In the Gospels themselves those closest to Jesus retain their own individuality even as they follow him. And those men and women throughout history who have been most successful in imitating Christ—the saints—have been one-of-a-kind individualists. Jesus ensured that there would be no mold to produce Christians. "If you love me, keep my word" is the only formula for Christ-likeness. It is an active, not a cosmetic, formula.

THE FRUITLESS QUEST

If the quest for the personality of Jesus is ultimately fruitless, it is nevertheless compelling. Christians have been motivated to seek after Jesus not simply from curiosity but because he is the door to God, the mediator between man and his Creator. To know Jesus is to know God. Rather than attempt to visualize an invisible God, the Christian at worship addresses Jesus, God's son, who is as real a human being as he or she is.

"Behold the man," proclaimed Pontius Pilate in displaying Jesus bound, beaten, and humiliated to the crowds who sought his death. Is this the real Jesus? At the close of the Dark Ages, with Europe in anarchy, the Man of Sorrows or Suffering Servant was the fashionable way of depicting the Savior. It was a way for Christians to focus on their sinfulness, as if to say, "This is what my sins did to God."

A similar mentality persists in some crucifixes in

contemporary Spain and Mexico, as well as those in the California mission churches founded by Spanish friars before the pilgrims landed at Plymouth Rock. During the high Middle Ages there was an inevitable reaction against the agonized Christ. St. Francis of Assisi shifted Christians' attention from Jesus' last painful moments to the beginnings of his life, presenting Jesus as the Babe of Bethlehem, the innocent child bringing light to the world. St. Francis inaugurated, a full millenium after Christ's birth, a reenactment of the journey to Bethlehem, using townspeople and a newborn infant as actors. In the saint's lifetime the Christmas pageant spread to nearly every village in Europe.

FASHIONS IN DEPICTING JESUS

After the Dark Ages, when Europe had returned to order and safety through the power of kings, a new cult developed. Jesus, the supreme ruler and lawgiver, was depicted as Christ the King, a conception of Christ that persists to this day despite the decline of monarchy. Even earlier, at the time of the transfer of the Roman Empire to Constantinople in what is now Turkey, Jesus was visualized as a ruler with Oriental trappings. In golden mosaic Jesus reigned over the world, as envisaged by the Byzantine emperors. This awesome conception of the severe sovereign persisted in the iconography of Russia until the Russian Revolution in our own century and has returned with the dismembering of the Soviet Union.

In Europe and America in recent times, churches and Christian homes have featured statues and lithographs of the Sacred Heart. As a conception of Jesus, it is a compromise between the suffering Christ of the final days, and the strong, compassionate Jesus in his prime. In this conception he displays, before his death, the heart that would be pierced for love of mankind.

The very earliest attempts to visualize Jesus are to be found in the Roman catacombs, underground burial places where early Christians also worshipped. Here Jesus is shown young, innocent, and clean-shaven, dressed in the Roman fashion. A more famous exception to our popular conception of the bearded and robed Jesus is contained in Michelangelo's vision of the Last Judgment, found in the Vatican's Sistine Chapel. Here Jesus meets the Renaissance requirements for heroic man. Christ floats in heaven on a cloud, a god-man of classical proportions. Michelangelo depicts Jesus with a nearly naked body of great strength. He rises from his throne, his face toward the damned. Christ's mother, close at his side, nevertheless shrinks from his wrath.

OTHER FASHIONS

Powerful as Michelangelo's conception of Judgment continues to be, the notion of an angry Jesus has never taken hold, although occasionally he is shown, in righteous wrath, casting the moneychangers from the Temple in Jerusalem. In a very different guise, Jesus is popularly depicted in a scene from the Gospels surrounded by children, blessing them. The kingdom of heaven is like a child, he says, referring to a child's openness, innocence, faith, devotion, and acceptance. A related conception is Jesus as head of the family, offering himself to the apostles in the forms of bread and wine, in the famous painting *The Last Supper* by Leonardo da Vinci. At the very opposite extreme from the Christ of *The Last Judgment* is the smiling Jesus, conceived by a recent illustrator, and popular in family Bibles and in some Christian homes.

The changing fashions for visualizing Jesus are never just whimsical; nevertheless they are only partially successful in conveying his personality. Although his message was simple, Christ's character is complex and rich.

There are those who would do away with imagery altogether. Protestant reformers, for example, removed Christ from the crucifix and made the cross a symbol. They made a point: Jesus is no longer suffering but is risen.

THE ADVANTAGES OF
VISUALIZING JESUS

While granting this point to the reformers, Orthodox and Catholic Christians prefer to keep the corpus on the cross lest it be forgotten that the Son of God was also a son of man. The great reformer Martin Luther retained statues, hymns, and illustrated stained-glass windows as aids to devotion. And family Bibles are routinely illustrated to emphasize that the Christian faith is based on a historical Jesus.

Although Christians are confident that they are heard by God, prayer is typically a one-sided conversation that is helped by the ability to visualize Jesus. Fortunately Jesus himself made references that are helpful. In a famous parable he spoke of a shepherd who leaves his flock to save the stray sheep: "I am the Good Shepherd; I know mine and mine know me." This image of Jesus is so powerful that many bishops continue to carry ceremonial staffs to remind Christians and themselves that they too must be good shepherds—caretakers of the faithful and sinners alike.

In another famous parable, Jesus identified himself with the forgiving father of the prodigal son, rejoicing in the return of the son who had previously abandoned him in favor of a life of dissipation.

Then there is the good Samaritan who goes out of his

way to care for a needy stranger after others had passed by
the wounded and impoverished man in their path. In
another place Jesus refers to himself as the "Light of the
World." In the one moment of glory he allowed himself in
his lifetime, Jesus was "transfigured" before his friends. The
Gospels speak of him as literally glowing with an inex-
tinguishable light.

There are other things we know of Jesus but which are
harder to visualize—that he was the Messiah, the Son of
God, Lord and Redeemer. Of his character, we know that
he was straightforward and compassionate. He was au-
thoritative. He accepted sinners but did not abide hypocrisy. He could love, and he could be roused to anger. He
possessed little and needed even less; yet he accepted
whatever was offered to him. Although Jesus knew fear, he
did not suffer the anxiety of indecision. Though he shrank
from pain, he was obedient unto death. In a moving scene,
Jesus demonstrated that sorrow is not weakness. When his
close friend Lazarus died, Jesus did not philosophize; he
wept.

Ironically, an important clue to Jesus' character comes
from an incident in which he was not recognized at all.
After his Resurrection he walked all day with two former
followers from Jerusalem to Emmaus. Although his appearance was altered, he was eventually recognized by them
from what he said and what he did. His companions knew
that this stranger was unique because when he spoke their
"hearts burned within them." Like those companions on

the road to Emmaus, Christians sometimes have had difficulty recognizing Jesus, but they have learned to love him because he is true to his words.

What Jesus taught

For twenty centuries Christians have echoed Jesus' own words in praying for God's kingdom to come, but with slight notion what it is they are asking for. Living as we do in a democracy, it is practically impossible to appreciate Jesus' thunderous and repeated message that a kingdom is at hand. What we know of kingdoms are quaint vestiges of former glories and tyrannies—royal families with no real authority acting as convenient figureheads.

The kingdom Jesus announced was nothing of the kind. His cousin, John the Baptist, had already sounded the alarm: "Reform your lives! The reign of God is at hand!" Jesus increased the urgency of this message, which became the cornerstone of his teaching. His appearance in history signaled the dawn of a new age that was irresistible. Heretofore, God had entered his universe only from time to time and for specific purposes. With Jesus, God joined creation totally and for all time.

Until the advent of Jesus, no one ever believed that God could take such an interest in his creation. With Jesus, God commits himself totally, even to the death. Jesus' announcement of the kingdom, therefore, was an unprecedented call for creation to respond to the love of its Creator: "Be perfect as your heavenly Father is perfect."

THE MEANING OF THE KINGDOM

The kingdom that Jesus announced had nothing to do with politics, although his enemies would kill him for fear that he would seize the government. What, then, was this kingdom? In many of his stories, Jesus seems to say that it will come slowly and imperceptibly. The kingdom, he says, is like a mustard seed—the smallest of seeds that yet has the capacity to develop into a great tree. Or, he says, it is like yeast folded into dough, causing it to rise into more than itself, becoming the breadloaf. In the same breath, Jesus insists that the kingdom is already here and present. "The Kingdom of God is in your midst," he tells his critics. Again, he stuns his enemies when he proclaims, "If it is by the Spirit of God that I expel demons, then the Kingdom of God has overtaken you!" Clearly, the kingdom is not fully apparent nor fully realized, but it has begun with Jesus.

Hence the relentless urgency of Jesus' preaching and the directness of his call. He would not ask anyone to follow him on a trial basis, but absolutely. When Jesus summoned fishermen to follow him as disciples, they not only dropped their nets, they dropped everything they were doing with their lives. For Jesus nothing is more precious than the kingdom. It is the perfect pearl for which a man sells everything he owns. As Jesus called to his disciples to leave all else to follow him, he called to everyone who heard him to prefer nothing to the kingdom.

The only acceptable response to the kingdom is a total change of heart—a transformation that builds upon repentance but exceeds it to include total surrender and active commitment. Jesus does not mince words. He demands that his hearers count the cost of accepting the kingdom. And he establishes the cost by forecasting his own death and the martyrdom of those who love him: "If a man wishes to come after me, he must deny his very self, take up his cross, and follow in my steps . . . Whoever would preserve his life will lose it, but whoever loses his life for my sake and the Gospel's will preserve it."

THE HEAD VERSUS THE HEART

If one is to accept and live in the kingdom, sentiment is insufficient. The head must lead the heart: "If one of you decides to build a tower, will he not first sit down and calculate the outlay to see if he has enough to complete the project?" When a man agreed to join Jesus on condition that he first bid farewell to his family, Jesus refuses him: "Whoever puts his hand to the plow but keeps looking back is unfit for the kingdom of God!"

No obstacle is to be allowed to compromise the primacy

of the kingdom in the lives of men and women—if hand or foot or eye is an obstacle, Jesus insists, "cut it off . . . gouge it out and cast it from you! Better to enter life crippled or with one eye." Those who make excuses rather than respond to the kingdom totally will forfeit life, Jesus says.

Comparing the kingdom to a king's banquet to whom all are invited but some send regrets, Jesus warns, "I tell you that not one of those invited shall taste a morsel of my dinner!" Jesus' call is not an invitation to sentimental consolation, nor an obscuring of the harsh facts of life and death. The Kingdom of God is God's decision for man, and it demands man's decision for God.

Jesus was not a persuader trying to bring people around to his way of thinking. He had nothing to sell, only something to give that demanded everything in return. Jesus was confronting people with their God and showing them how to respond to God—as Jesus did, by obedience. In his own response to God, Jesus' only advantage over other men and women was that he was not alienated from his Creator. He was not simply God in human form, but a human being who had to learn about God, only gradually coming to realize the fullness of that divine nature within him.

WHAT JESUS LEARNED

From childhood, Jesus learned about God in the same manner as his fellow Jews—from reading Scripture and listening to rabbis in the synagogues. He learned as well from prayer in public and in private. With his countrymen, Jesus daily recited the Shema: "Hear, O Israel, the Lord is our God, the Lord alone! Therefore you shall love the Lord, our God, with all your heart, with all your soul, and with all your strength."

Jesus grew to adulthood learning through Scripture of God's love for his people, of God's expectations of his people, and of his promise to them. When Jesus began his ministry as an adult, he demonstrated that his mission was remarkable not for some strange novelty that he might open up to the world, but for the simple fact that his task was to lay out the expectations God had of ordinary men and women. Jesus was not responding to any hidden agenda of God but to God's expectations clearly stated in Scripture for everyone to read.

What was unique and radical about Jesus was not his invention of new teachings about God, but his compelling restatement of God's plan and his total obedience to what God had already told the Jews. Throughout his ministry, Jesus quoted Scripture against his self-righteous critics, claiming that what he did fulfilled the Scripture.

This was not just a clever ploy to put off his critics. By quoting Scripture, Jesus was putting everyone on the spot: "I do the will of God, why don't you?" But Jesus did not simply quote Scripture nor assume the posture of a faithful prophet. He clearly spoke with an authority that came from a special relationship with God that was confirmed at the outset of his ministry. We cannot guess how Jesus arrived at the conviction that he was called to proclaim

God's kingdom. But at his baptism by John, his ministry was confirmed by God himself: "This is my beloved Son; my favor rests on him."

GOD, MY FATHER

Jesus, in turn, calls God Father, not in the sense of Creator, but in the sense of his own loving Father, and ours. When Jesus prayed he called God "Abba" with the same intimate familiarity as we call our fathers "Dad" or "Daddy." In the story of the Prodigal Son, Jesus explains the kind of father God is. In his story, the father runs to meet his wayward son, embracing and kissing him and preparing a feast to celebrate his return. This is the God Jesus knows and emulates: a Father who loves and forgives in total generosity. For this reason Jesus can say: "When you see me, you see the Father." God's love is indiscriminate, and Jesus loves just as indiscriminately, even to death. It is his intimate experience of a loving God that lends Jesus' teaching the appearance of novelty when in fact it is only articulate, single-minded, and rigorously conclusive.

The Jews already knew that the two great commandments were to love God and neighbor. But Jesus pressed the commandment to the logical conclusion that sprang from his intimate knowledge that God is love itself. Jesus insisted that we must love precisely as God loves—democratically and indiscriminately—including our enemies, those who repel us, and those to whom we are indifferent. <u>The ability to forgive is the key to the King-dom of God because it tests the genuineness of our love.</u> It is no accident that in the Lord's Prayer, in which Jesus' followers call for the kingdom to come, they add "Forgive us the wrong we have done, as we forgive those who wrong us."

Jesus sealed this message with the story of a king who forgives a servant's enormous debt only to learn later that the servant refused to forgive a much smaller debt owed him by a fellow servant. Recalling the servant, the master says, "I canceled your entire debt when you pleaded with me. Should you not have dealt mercifully with your fellow servant, as I dealt with you?" In Jesus' story, the master reinstates the debt, and Jesus concludes: "My heavenly Father will treat you in exactly the same way unless each of you forgives his brother from his heart."

LOVE VERSUS RULEKEEPING

When he called for a love based on generosity and for-giveness, Jesus found himself at odds with Jewish authori-ties who had adopted the mentality that mere faithfulness to rules was equivalent to love. Time and again Jesus challenged the hypocrisy of the rule-keepers and showy do-gooders. As a Jew himself, Jesus upheld the religious laws and practices of the Jews, but only as they expressed a fundamental loving forgiveness in each person. In the last discourse recorded by St. John, Jesus summarized his teaching:

> As the Father has loved me, so have I loved you; abide in my love. If you keep my commandments, you will abide in my love, just I have kept my Father's commandments and abide in his love.
>
> These things I have spoken to you, that my joy may be in you, and that your joy may be full.
>
> This is my commandment, that you love one another as I have loved you.
>
> (JOHN 15:9–12)

The prologue to the Gospel of St. John remains the most concise and poetic expression of Jesus' identity as Son of God, his preexistence as God's Word, and his work of redemption:

> In the beginning was the Word and the Word was with God, and the Word was God. He was in the beginning with God; all things were made through him, and without him was not anything made that was made. In him was life, and the life was the light of men. The light shines in the darkness, and the darkness has not overcome it.
>
> There was a man sent from God, whose name was

John. He came for testimony, to bear witness to the light, that all might believe through him. He was not the light, but came to bear witness to the light.

The true light that enlightens every man was coming into the world. He was in the world, and the world was made through him, yet the world knew him not. He came to his own home, and his own people received him not. But to all who received him, who believed in his name, he gave power to become children of God; who were born, not of blood nor of the will of the flesh nor of the will of man, but of God.

And the Word became flesh and dwelt among us, full of grace and truth; we have beheld his glory, glory as of the only Son from the Father.

(JOHN 1:1–14)

QUESTIONS FOR DISCUSSION OR SELF-STUDY:

1. What is the significance of Jesus being a Jew?

2. How did Jesus fulfill and modify the old Covenant?

3. What did Jesus mean by the Kingdom of God on earth?

4. Why does every generation attempt to "reinvent" Jesus?

5. What is the law of love?

CHAPTER 4

THE GOOD LIFE

A RADICAL MISCONCEPTION

Nothing so deters the reluctant Christian from embarking on a life of faith as the fear that he or she must begin living a life of impossible virtue contrary to all his or her inclinations. Unhappily, this is a gross misconception of Christianity contrived by those who would substitute shame and the fear of God for love and forgiveness as life's motives. It is wrong.

In point of fact, the hardest part of being a Christian is faith, not morality—believing, not behaving. Alone of the world's great faiths Christianity clearly subordinates behavior to belief and it radically replaces rulekeeping and ritual observance with the single, all-embracing motive of love. It is impossible to be a "righteous" Christian. No matter how faithful the follower, he remains flawed, needing God's forgiveness. The rule of love is so radical that no one scores 100 percent or can give himself even a passing grade. That is God's gift.

God is more forgiving and less demanding than governments, institutions, neighbors, or families. Reflect how Moses' succinct Ten Commandments pale before the following:

—a legal code so extensive it requires a library in every attorney's office
—the countless covenants that govern the behavior of nations and even the smallest communities
—the private restrictions and bylaws conceived by corporations and institutions of every kind
—the complex spoken and unspoken behavioral expectations that exist in every family and personal relationship.

It is not religion that seeks to rule our lives, telling us what is criminal and shameful. Rather, it is the law and other people, both friends and strangers. Basic "good behavior" is nothing more nor less than civility driven by habit and aided by conscience. There is no escaping it whatever one's religion or lack of faith without suffering prosecution or the enmity of neighbors and loved ones. Christianity, far from placing a moral burden on the reluctant Christian, relieves the weight of one that is already there, lightening it by the addition of love and forgiveness. The life of faith adds not constraint, but freedom—the "freedom of the sons of God."

ONLY GOD IS GOOD

Whatever else people may think of him, Jesus is universally acclaimed as a great moral teacher. Consequently there is a perennial temptation to identify Christianity with an ethical or moral system—a regimen for good behavior or the good life. In fact, <u>Christianity pays only subordinate attention to mankind's ethical activity, concentrating instead on the activity of God</u>. Rather than building religion on a prescribed human behavior toward God, Christianity builds on God's behavior toward man.

This makes all the difference in the world. As Jesus himself noted, "Only God is good." It is God's graciousness, not mankind's righteousness, that is the foundation of the Christian religion. The Old Testament of the Jews was a chronicle of God's faithfulness and mankind's faithlessness. The Good News of Jesus Christ is that God so loved the world that he offered his Son to take our place and save us from ourselves. This saving initiative belongs wholly to God; no man, woman, or child can merit salvation. That explains why Jesus constantly exposed the hypocrisy of religious leaders who pretended that good behavior alone earned God's favor.

Only the obedience unto death of God's own Son was sufficient to summon God's saving love. Jesus alone was the perfectly faithful human being. In response, Christians seek to imitate Jesus, motivated by love alone, not because good behavior will win them a prize. Jesus is our prize.

Jesus told story after story illustrating that God loves not only the just but the sinner. The Good Shepherd leaves his flock to find the one lamb that is lost. The faithful father rushes to embrace his prodigal son. Again and again Jesus teaches that it is responsiveness to God's generosity that counts. He calls for a change of heart, not for rigid righteousness. In Islam and Judaism, by contrast, strict attention to religious duty wins God's favor: man acts and God responds. Morality for the Christian is the absolute reverse—a loving response to a loving God. God acts, and man responds.

G R O W I N G   I N   L O V E

Although Christianity assumes the chronic sinfulness of mankind, it insists on man's ability to grow in love. The allegory of the Garden of Eden illustrates the original peace between God and his creation. Paradise was God and man at peace. Eden ended when Adam and Eve became bored with being only human and began to idolize themselves, excluding God, then mistrusting one another. The Old Testament chronicles God's subsequent attempts to overcome our inherited alienation and to restore our peace with God, with our fellowman, and with ourselves. The Old Testament allegories of the Tower of Babel and

Noah and the Flood illustrate mankind's continued perversity and powerlessness without God. With Abraham, forebear of the Jewish people, God intervened again, this time to establish a covenant with the Jews expressing his intention to renew the peace of paradise. God's demands were few yet his Chosen People continued to falter.

Through Moses some twelve centuries before Christ, God further specified the terms of faithfulness to his Covenant. The Ten Commandments, if observed, might not physically recreate paradise, but they would repair the peace of man with God and man with man. The commandments called for respect for God and family. Moreover, by prohibiting murder, theft, adultery, and falsehood, they confronted our perennial obstacles to peace. As the Old Testament chronology unfolded, Moses' original commandments were elaborated and prophets emerged in every generation to remind the Jews that it was not fidelity to rules but faithfulness to God that was the purpose of the covenant.

BREAKING THE RULES

Jesus was notorious for breaking rules to dramatize their essential function as guidelines for a loving response to God's offer of peace. He healed on the Sabbath. He scandalized religious leaders by dining with sinners. He challenged those who attempted to execute an adulteress, inviting "whoever is without sin" to cast the first stone. Jesus was a scandal to the literal-minded, who conveniently divided men and women into good and evil based on their public behavior. As Jesus explained it, everyone is handicapped because all are sinners. At the same time everyone is fundamentally good by dint of God loving them. God can only love what is good. When rules get between God and man, and man and man, they are useless and even harmful. Jesus' underlying commandment—to love—is too fundamental to be classified as a rule. The demands of love are greater than any mere set of prescriptions.

Jesus taught that love is humble, poor, peaceful, and patient. Love embraces everyone and extends to strangers, to enemies, and to persecutors. Exemplifying the love he preached, Jesus died at the hands of his "righteous" enemies so that mankind might live reconciled with God. As he drew his final breath, Jesus predictably forgave his own executioners.

The small, primitive Christian communities of the first century attempted literally to imitate the example of Jesus and largely succeeded in restoring a semblance of Eden. Christian families lived simply, pooling their possessions and giving away any excess to the poor. They fasted and prayed, patiently awaiting the return of Jesus which they mistakenly thought to be imminent. They lived in peace, exemplifying the love of God and man. What was realistic for these small persecuted communities of believers, of course, could not be applied to Christian life once Christianity became the faith of empire. Virtues appropriate for close family and community living are not blindly applicable to a Christian's responsibilities in the wider world. Civil and economic rights, commerce, and war present moral dimensions that resist a simplistic application of the law of love.

Unfortunately, Jesus himself offered little practical advice for dealing with major social problems. The law of love has to be combined with the education of conscience. Early Christian writers referred to this development as "the way of wisdom."

FROM PERSONAL TO SOCIAL MORALITY

In the Old Testament what appears to be a justification for revenge ("eye for eye; tooth for tooth") was actually a moral advance over the prevailing practice of the avenger to kill for the merest slight or injury. Jesus went much further, not only forbidding revenge, but appealing to his followers to love their enemies. In practice, many Christians who seek to follow Jesus' counsel in their private lives also support wars, prisons, and capital punishment in the larger world. They point to Jesus, who counseled soldiers to obey their officers and called upon everyone's duty to government ("Render to Caesar the things that are Caesar's"). A devoted minority of Christians to this day, however, insist that nations as well as individuals are bound equally by the Sermon on the Mount.

Inevitably, even the most motivated Christian wrestles with his tendency to set his own will against God's and is not always certain in a complex world which way is the way of love. Without approving slavery as an institution, for example, St. Paul called on slaves to obey their masters. And Christianity for centuries—and for practical reasons—accepted a society of vast inequities and cruel punishments. Only in very recent times has one's social conscience been confronted with demands that clearly break with Christian tradition. In the United States, for example, abortion—long unchallenged as infanticide— has been legalized for humanitarian reasons favoring women. Traditional conscience interprets the law of love as weighing more for the survival of the child than for the convenience of its mother. But not all Christians agree.

In any event, the law of love for the Christian is much more than mere humanitarianism and is utterly unsenti- mental. Christians reject the secular humanist notion that man is the measure of all things. Christians respond that God is. The Christian loves his fellowman precisely be- cause God loves every creature. Christ's personal sacrifice for mankind is painful proof of the value of every man, woman, and child in God's sight.

LOVE AND CONSTRAINT

The law of love proceeds from freedom, not from constraint. St. Paul proclaimed "the freedom of the glory of the sons of God." Without a trace of irony St. Paul could tell Christians to "love, and do what you will," knowing that Christ's followers would not interpret freedom as license but as an invitation to do as Jesus did. Salvation for the Christian is not deferred to an afterlife; the Christian is unburdened of sin now and is free to follow Jesus. Whereas the Jews associated faithfulness to God with the observance of taboos, St. Paul insists that nothing is "unclean" for the Christian who is free to allow Christ to act within him.

Sin is not inevitable; it is only unreasonable and unloving. Classical writers defined sin as missing the mark—an indulgence in blindness and delusion. Sin is idolatrous, a travesty in which a creature of God perversely pretends to be God. The most obvious sins are, of course, abusive of others. Civilized societies protect themselves from the most serious abuses by means of laws and punishments for offenders. But the most insidious thing about sin short of crime is that it is self-destructive. Indeed, many persons who are not dangerous to anyone else abuse themselves through drugs or drink, overwork or sensuality. Christians regard suicide as the ultimate abuse of self and the ultimate denial of God's love and care.

Sin is often not abusive at all but simply indifferent. Dante filled the great entrance hall to his allegorical Hell with people whose sin consisted of paying insufficient attention and not caring. For the Christian love is never neutral or passive; it is always giving. Jesus' Sermon on the Mount is notable for its absence of prohibitions. Instead Jesus calls for positive initiative through responsible love— make peace, feed the hungry, share with the poor, care for the sick. Only in recent times has government assumed some responsibility for the needy. Such care in Christian countries is still dominated by religious institutions.

The Christian is not a sentimental do-gooder, nor is he or she a humanitarian who loves mankind in the abstract but cannot abide real individuals. Christianity has no monopoly on morality but it possesses a unique motive. It finds dignity in the down-and-out. It despairs of no individual, knowing that the Son of God died for every person in history. The lesson is clear. If God became man because of love, then man can approach the perfection of God by following Christ. The secret is to say yes to Jesus' invitation: "Follow me."

CATS ARE NOT CHRISTIANS

My family's three cats are object lessons in natural, amoral behavior, so let us examine them. Each has his or her own personality, to be sure, but Brutus, Sheba, and Oreo are alike in being creatures of instinct—which seems to serve them well except for getting out of the way of moving automobiles. The cats sleep, eat, purr, lick themselves, and hiss at our Scottish Terrier. The youngest, Oreo, also hunts moles, frogs, and baby birds, and presents us proudly with his carnage. Oreo is an affectionate pet but he is no Christian.

That is to say, Oreo never has second thoughts. He does not question what is expected of him or ponder whether he has done the right thing. In short, he has instinct and affection but no conscience. In contrast, our dog has an artificial sense of shame and will crawl into a dark bathroom when she has done something that we must clean off a carpet. But she, like the cats, lacks an ethical sense; she is only sensitive to our displeasure and prefers to punish herself before we think of something more drastic.

It is only men, women, and children who agonize over whether they have done the right thing. People are constantly judging themselves and each other ethically. It is a high compliment to be thought of as a good person.

ARE CHILDREN ANIMALS?

Children can be compared to laboratory animals because they are constantly having their behavior scrutinized by adults. Lacking the instincts that equip our cats for independence and survival, the human child is dependent physically on its parents. A child's natural behavior may occasionally be judged cute, but it is inadequate both for survival in nature and in the company of adults. Children are often forgiven for bad behavior, but essential to the process of maturation is developing a child's conscience so he or she can make judgments about appropriate behavior. The alternative to good conscience is prison, where someone else makes all the decisions and keeps criminal adults in a perpetual state of childhood.

THE ATTRACTION OF EVIL

If we had to pass our lives making ethical decisions from moment to moment we would go mad. Scrupulosity is the moral equivalent of hypochondria. Fortunately, in lieu of animal instinct people have habit. As I write this on a summer morning, I have been awake for two hours and doubt that I have accomplished anything of moral significance. Rather, everything I did was mechanical, from washing my face to feeding the pets and catching my bus. Nor do I anticipate any great moral decisions in the day ahead. Does this mean that I am neither good nor bad?

Good and evil are not just judgments about behavior but about things and people. To call an automobile good or a painting bad says something about their character. It can be a good car even when it is parked with the motor off or a bad painting even when it is hidden away in the attic. Similarly, we assess people's character even when they are not actually doing something heroic or horrid. In this respect on this morally indifferent Wednesday, my enemies will still despise me and my friends will think well of me whether I do anything at all to prompt their judgment.

A life of habit and routine is not very interesting for people. An animal does not willingly introduce additional conflict into its life, but people do it all the time to escape boredom and—ironically—to create the illusion of being in control. Often the conflict we add is vicarious. As if life is not competitive enough and full of rules, we create sports, establishing new rules and artificial challenges. We manufacture theater and fiction to provide ourselves with suspense, passion, murder, mayhem, love, loss, alienation, and reconciliation that distract us from our relatively safe but dull lives of habit. Another creation—politics—is part sport, part theater, but equally a way of contriving conflict to make life more interesting.

Most people are, in point of fact, ethical junkies. We love being in a world where good and evil are in conflict, where choices must be made for gain or loss. Everyone loves a villain because he represents this drama in its purest form. We all, more or less, attempt to be good but come up short, which is unsatisfying. How much more interesting to contemplate being absolutely consistent— to be evil!

HOW BAD IS BAD?

But even villainy is inconsistent. Shakespeare's Iago was at least honest with his audience, and Hitler was kind to his dogs. Villainy takes a lot of mental and physical effort and persistent attention. Evil is much more than simple selfishness (which after all is what characterizes animals and small children). Rather, evil is malicious, cruel, and contrived. It does not seek satisfaction but destruction. In this respect, most of us are not very evil. Even in our vilest moods we tend to be hapless villains, setting fire to our own neighborhoods, breaking our own dishes, and berating the people who love us most. We are usually the victims of our own moral lapses.

My own father, who had a temper but was ordinarily the mildest and kindest of men, insisted that it was only Christianity that kept him from being a rake and reprobate. In retrospect, I believe that he simply kept in check a fondness for women other than my mother and refrained from joining his co-workers at a bar on the way home from work. His frustrations were real and his temptations common to his fellowmen, but even without his Christian faith my father would probably have lived the sober, faithful, loving life he in fact did live.

CIVIC VIRTUE AND THE
CIVIL LAW

There was virtue and vice before there was Christianity, so we must be careful to identify what is expected of us independent of religion. Normally we appraise appropriate behavior in ourselves and others by reference to the civic virtues, not by uniquely Christian goodness. We expect ourselves and others to be fair, truthful, courteous, sober, patriotic, and responsible to family and community. These were the ethical expectations of the pagan Romans, who established the laws and created the larger civilization into which Jesus himself was born. When Jesus told his followers to "render to Caesar the things that are Caesar's," he was upholding the civil law and civic virtue. There is nothing especially Christian about them; they are basic to civilized behavior.

The civic virtues, while basic, require more than simple law abiding. There are plenty of unvirtuous people who manage to stay out of jail; laws express only the most basic expectations that people in community have of one another. I do not want to buy a used car from someone who only obeys statutes on the law books and thereby keeps himself from a jail cell. I want someone I can trust: in short, a virtuous car dealer, but not necessarily a religious or Christian one.

IS MORALITY RELATIVE?

It is sophomoric to dismiss morality as merely traditional or fashionable behavior. Morality is not etiquette. It is behavior that society recognizes as responsible and therefore vital for any kind of predictable, let alone civilized living. Laws protect us from destructive behavior; the civic virtues make us act responsibly whatever the vagaries of the times or the society we happen to live in.

Morality "changes" only in the sense that people develop more sophisticated consciences. What evolves is our sense of what responsible behavior is. The notion of responsibility does not change; it defines what we owe to one another. As time goes by we tend to demand more responsibility from one another.

One hundred and fifty years ago in the American South many people considered it moral to own slaves. There were "good" slaveholders and "bad" slaveholders, the difference being how humanely the owners treated their human property. Today we consider it self-evident that the very notion of human ownership is evil in itself, but in that time many owners felt that slavery was not only an economic necessity but that it was the only institution that provided for responsible care for black Americans.

Did the morality of slavery "change" with its abolition? Historically, it simply become more and more evident that the institution was flawed and open to actual and widespread abuse. The institution was unmasked as irresponsible, so consciences were educated to the fact. Morality did not change, but people's sense of civilized and responsible behavior did.

At the present time there is a similar dispute about the morality of capital punishment. Jesus himself inveighed against the vengeful behavior that had been permitted in the Judaism of his time. But at the present time those who resist the death penalty as immoral do so not for religious reasons at all but for civic ones. Again as in the case of slavery, the controlling consideration is factual (Does capital punishment deter crime?) and responsible (Is capital punishment itself murder?). However we settle this matter, fifty years from now people will wonder how we could have been so morally obtuse not to realize what was expected as good, decent behavior. We are similarly divided as a society on the responsibility of gun ownership, but a moral consensus will probably be driven by the accumulation of experience about the effect of guns on the streets.

The present generation continues to change its sense of responsible behavior, but that fact alone does not make morality relative. There is nothing magical about morality; morality makes sense and protects people. When I was younger, I smoked cigarettes. Now evidence suggests that the practice, then considered innocent, is unhealthy for the smoker and for those around him. Here is a case where, as with slavery, we have not only sharpened our ethical sense but have passed new laws defining responsible behavior.

As I write this, the nation is in a political campaign that has contrasted individual freedom with family values. That a nation's people lack complete consensus does not mean that moral imperatives have lost their force. Rather, it reflects our consciences grappling with better information and new concerns about our responsibility to ourselves and one another. A better-informed conscience, however, does not guarantee good behavior.

IS ANY BEHAVIOR PURELY PERSONAL?

A whole array of behavior once thought to be irresponsible and damaging to society is now considered by some to be personal, not social at all. The practice of open homosexuality, contraception, abortion, and other behaviors stemming from the sexual revolution of the 1960s suggests that what was once immoral is now acceptable. That is not the case. What is argued (in civic, not religious terms) is that some kinds of behavior ought not to be judged as responsible or irresponsible because they are purely personal.

Those who advocate allowing the terminally ill to decide when to end their lives make their case on the same basis—that suffering is personal and that suicide is none of society's business. At the moment, euthanasia as a purely private matter confronts obstacles. Ending one's life during an illness usually requires assistance. Moreover, family members constitute a small "society" that could maintain the life of a loved one. But euthanasia is in the air.

Many persons are appalled and offended by new behaviors that are justified as "purely personal." In the United States the Bill of Rights protects a great deal of behavior that is bizarre and distasteful. But to tolerate does not means to sanction or admire. Remember, we are speaking only of civic morality with no religious dimension. What has "changed" is that some behaviors are proposed strictly in terms of one's responsibility to oneself, not to others. Whether an abortion or mercy-killing is worthy of the individual or does any good is another question altogether, but morality is not thereby made relative. The principal ethical imperative of responsibility remains. We are creatures of conscience rather than instinct, and conscience is not instinctive. It is not only difficult to do some things we ought to do, but it is often difficult to know precisely what they are.

In some instances society today defines an individual's responsibility to himself. Seat belts must be worn by drivers and helmets by motorcyclists. Many untested and nearly all mood-altering drugs are prohibited to individuals by law. This is not an exception to civic morality's function to require social responsibility. Rather, government (speaking for society) is saying that there are private behaviors that have clear public implications and must be regulated. The individual must be "protected from himself," otherwise society will suffer. If a motorcyclist crashes without a helmet, for example, it is society that must scrape him off the pavement and care for a brain-damaged cripple. Smokers' rights were once defended as a personal option until society (in the person of those in the vicinity of the smoker) complained that it was impossible for anyone to smoke without affecting everyone around him.

A RECAPITULATION

Before moving on from mere civility to behavior that is religiously motivated, let us recapitulate. Although all men and women have values that give their lives direction, most of what we do is by rote and habit, and even many of our practical judgments (Do I turn left or right to get to Chicago?) are not by nature the subject of morality. Morality predates religion and is based on responsibility to oneself and one's society. It is not relative. No society claims that the right thing to do is to lie, murder, cheat, or to abandon one's family. What appears to be changing as time passes is better described as a sharper sense of the impact of personal behavior on others and what our responsibility to one another involves. What is merely allowed or not strictly prohibited is not by that fact good. We can manage to stay out of prison by superficial attention to law, but we cannot escape the pervasive moral judgment of other people who appraise our character by what we do and fail to do and who have their own ways of punishing us. Good behavior, in short, makes good sense, but it is not necessarily idealistic or compassionate, and of itself is unrelated to religious faith.

QUESTIONS FOR DISCUSSION OR SELF-STUDY:

1. Morally, what distinguishes humans from other creatures?

2. Where does good behavior end and Christian behavior begin?

3. Which is worse: evil or indifference?

4. Why is love the all-encompassing rule of life for the Christian?

5. Is morality different for nations and institutions than for individuals?

CHAPTER 5

THE LIFE OF LOVE

"FOLLOW ME"

Society insists that we follow the law. Institutions demand that we follow rules and procedures. Neighbors and families call on us to follow their expectations. Jesus says simply: "Follow me."

At the time he walked the earth he meant it literally—drop what you are doing and follow me wherever I go. Two thousand years later he still wishes us to drop our preoccupations, shift our priorities, and unburden and personalize our approach to life. "Conversion" literally means "turning around." Turning around quickly can make one dizzy at first, but following Jesus is a dizzying reorientation of one's life. Others may not note your transformation as a man or woman of faith. You will not thereby lose your weaknesses, but only allow yourself to be forgiven. You will not go from indifferent to exemplary behavior. A

Christian, because he is human, is always handicapped. But you will sense your change because you will see life more simply and vividly and begin to act from the simple motive of love.

ADDING THE RELIGIOUS DIMENSION TO GOOD BEHAVIOR

Religious morality does not contradict the moral imperatives that bind all peoples at all times, but it adds a dimension of personal responsibility toward God. We must be careful not to fall into the trap of telling our children that they must be good "because God is watching." We must be good because we are in fact responsible to ourselves and to others.

But it is possible to be motivated in all our behavior by our love of God. Devout Christians dedicate all that they do, from washing dishes to working in a soup kitchen, to God. In the process morally indifferent acts are infused with significance because they become a loving response to a loving God. Similarly, the mundane chores in a marriage are, taken together, expressions of devotion to the person one lives with. They may not be heroic or even difficult, but their consistency and cumulative value bespeak devotion, which motivates everything one does and offers transcendence to our routines.

In the Old Testament God proves again and again his

faithfulness to the people of Israel but requires them to prove their own faithfulness in return. The cumulative story is of some success and much failure on man's part, balanced by the patient persistence of God. God requires some ritual observances by the Jews, but these must not be mistaken for moral imperatives. Rather, they are reminders of faithfulness to him. Dietary restrictions, sacrifices, and circumcision are signs of membership—of belonging to God.

The commandments given to Moses about twelve centuries before Christ for the Jewish people are clear moral imperatives. Here they are as they appear in the Book of Exodus Chapter 20:

And God spoke all these words, saying, "I am the Lord your God, who brought you out of the land of Egypt, out of the house of bondage.

"You shall have no other gods before me.

"You shall not make for yourself a graven image, or any likeness of anything that is in heaven above, or that is in the earth beneath, or that is in the water under the earth; you shall not bow down to them or serve them; for I the Lord your God am a jealous God, visiting the iniquity of the fathers upon the children to the third and the fourth generation of those who hate me, but showing steadfast love to thousands of those who love me and keep my commandments.

"You shall not take the name of the Lord your God in

vain; for the Lord will not hold him guiltless who takes his name in vain.

"Remember the sabbath day, to keep it holy. Six days you shall labor, and do all your work; but the seventh day is a sabbath to the Lord your God; in it you shall not do any work, you, or your son, or your daughter, your manservant, or your maidservant, or your cattle, or your sojourner who is within your gates; for in six days the Lord made heaven and earth, the sea, and all that is in them, and rested the seventh day; therefore the Lord blessed the sabbath day and hallowed it.

"Honor your father and your mother, that your days may be long in the land which the Lord your God gives you.

"You shall not kill.

"You shall not commit adultery.

"You shall not steal.

"You shall not bear false witness against your neighbor.

"You shall not covet your neighbor's house; you shall not covet your neighbor's wife, or his manservant, or his maidservant, or his ox, or his ass, or anything that is your neighbor's."

(EXODUS 20: 1–17)

Half of the commandments define our relationship with God; the remainder deal with our responsibility to one another. These latter commandments, though revealed by

God to the Jews, are not exactly surprises. They restate, with God's authority, the conventional (or civic) requirements of social responsibility.

There is nothing here exclusive to the Jews. Who can argue with prohibitions against murder, libel, theft, adultery, and poaching—or with respect for parents? God here is putting the force of his own authority behind what a semicivilized people already knew in their hearts was expected of them.

The first half of the commandments is something else altogether. Here God states his own claims over his people, demanding exclusive devotion and honesty from them, and even a day each week of their time. God insists that he is personal; no fetishes or idols will be allowed to interfere with the requirement that each person deal with him, worship him alone.

THE RELUCTANT CHRISTIAN VERSUS THE COMMANDMENTS

Clearly half the commandments coincide with conscience and do not require God's revelation. A nonbeliever is equally required to obey them. <u>What God demands</u> of those who believe in him, however, is something much more, namely that we love him.

The reluctant believer is justified in balking at being forced to love anyone. How can love be commanded? On a purely human level, it probably cannot, although many men and women inexplicably continue to love those who treat them badly. But in God's case, he is by definition lovable: always giving and forgiving, always faithful, always responsible, never perverse or forgetful. Since we are designed by God to be fulfilled by him, love is the only appropriate relationship.

Then why must love be commanded? Because people are perverse, and the first sign of perversity is forgetfulness and indifference. The Old Testament is a chronicle of God's faithfulness and mankind's indifference. That helps to explain why God comes across as so demanding. He is trying to get and sustain our attention. Is he an angry God? Yes, if anger will get our attention. Does he punish the unfaithful? Yes, but only to bring us to our senses and to our destiny. The prototypical story in the Old Testament depicts the first man and woman cared for by God yet tempted to become independent of him. The forbidden fruit they choose is self-will and indifference. An angry God deports them from paradise but does not abandon them. The continuing story is of a faithful God taking initiatives to mend the breach caused by mankind, finally restoring it through his Son, Jesus, who was faithful unto death.

THE MORALITY OF JESUS

Jesus' Sermon on the Mount represents an unprecedented leap from the commandments given to Moses to a point far beyond. Whereas the prohibitions against murder, libel, theft, adultery, and covetousness could be deduced by any reasonable man or woman, believer or not, Jesus' expectations are radical departures from any purely "reasonable" good behavior. Although Jesus does not contradict Moses' commandments, his own revelation is not a development or evolution of them but a new way of behaving.

The Mosaic law, for example, permitted justice proportionate to the offense. "Eye for eye, tooth for tooth" sounds uncivilized, but it was a great improvement on the tendency to overreaction. Duelists would kill to avenge an insult. I would want to kill anyone who molested my wife or children. The Old Law would not have restrained me.

But Jesus does not allow us to respond to aggression with aggression. "You have heard that it was said, 'You shall love your neighbor and hate your enemy.' But I say to you, love your enemies and pray for those who persecute you." Jesus praises poverty—not just simplicity "in spirit"—but simple living, and warns repeatedly of the distractions of wealth. He makes sorrow, suffering, and meekness into virtues, but he does not preach passivity. Rather we are to be pure-hearted peacemakers, to promote what is right, to show mercy.

This is a bewildering agenda and a prescription for behavior that, unlike reasonable morality, goes utterly against the grain. Even our educated consciences tell us that poverty is evil and that loving our enemies is a prescription for disaster. How can we be Christians if we not only don't follow Jesus' way but believe his way is unreasonable?

HOW REALISTIC ARE JESUS' EXPECTATIONS?

Before we are tempted to dismiss Jesus' expectations of us as unreasonable and impractical, let us acknowledge that he followed them himself. Even at death's door, fixed by nails to a cross, he continued to project the image of a single-minded man in control of his destiny. He did not fold; he prevailed. Far from being a passive victim, Jesus led a life of heroic integrity.

Even in the best of times most Christian preachers do not bother much with the Sermon on the Mount, preferring to deal with what may seem to be more basic morality. They reason that it is more important to appeal for honesty and against self-indulgence, thus inspiring some generosity among the faithful. Preachers do not think of this as minimalism but as no-frills appeals to responsible behavior. Why press a man to love his enemy when he does not do well enough by his wife and children?

The Sermon on the Mount is not exactly dismissed as hopelessly idealistic by theologians and church leaders; it is viewed as so advanced as to apply to saints, not to average Christians. Practically speaking, many are inclined to argue that Jesus was a special case, not only by reason of who he was, but because he did not have the responsibilities of fixed employment, a mortgage, a wife, and children. He, unlike us, was free to lead a life of hardship, sacrifice, and vulnerability. Jesus, by this way of thinking, was not street-smart but we must be.

How, then, is the reluctant Christian to respond to Jesus' invitation: "Follow me?"

THE "FOOLISHNESS" OF ACTING AS A CHRISTIAN

I suggest that our reluctance to respond to Jesus stems not from any disagreement with him but from a fear of going out on a limb, of trying and falling flat. We hate the prospect of appearing foolish. If we're going to try to act like Christians, we don't want to appear amateurish about it, but that appears to be the best we can expect from ourselves since Jesus' standards are Olympian!

One way to gain perspective is to examine those very ordinary first followers of Jesus to see how they handled Jesus' "impossible" demands. With rare exceptions the twelve apostles were uneducated and unsophisticated. The

Gospels do not make them out to be heroes; rather, they graphically illustrate instances of their cowardice, sloth, lying, vanity, envy, indifference, and narrow-mindedness. Yet Jesus chose these all-too-human men to carry his message and to create an institutional church that even in their brief lifetimes extended throughout most of the civilized world. Why were these men, so much less sophisticated than we, not deterred by Jesus' demands of moral perfection?

The answer is not simple, yet it is the key to the reluctant Christian's decision to follow Jesus. Flawed as they were, the apostles were true friends to Jesus. They wavered, but they were faithful. They did in fact follow Jesus physically, but that was only an indication that they had already thrown in their lot with him. They trusted him and entrusted themselves to him, confident that he would make it possible for them to do anything he demanded of them. Judas, the one apostle who lost faith in Jesus, so despaired of his betrayal that he hanged himself.

This faithful behavior of the apostles is far from perfection, but it is grounded in the commitment that sets the reluctant Christian solidly on the path to perfection. It is not unlike the husband who is faithful to his wife because he realizes she is faithful to him and necessary for his happiness. Such a husband is neither perfect man nor perfect husband, but he is clearly committed and single-minded. He knows where his heart is. That is what Jesus wants from us. Once we have made a basic, personal commitment, the rest falls into place.

St. Paul, the one apostle who did not have the privilege of knowing Jesus in life, cautioned Christians that they could not escape acting foolishly, because their leader had already chosen the ultimate folly—to be the victim of his own creatures and to die for love of them:

> For the foolishness of God is wiser than
> men, and the weakness of God is stronger than
> men.
> For consider your call, brethren; not many
> of you were wise according to worldly standards,
> not many were powerful, not many were of noble
> birth; but God chose what is foolish in the
> world to shame the wise. God chose what is
> weak in the world to shame the strong. God chose
> what is low and despised in the world, even
> things that are not, to bring to nothing things
> that are, so that no human being might boast in
> the presence of God.
>
> (1 CORINTHIANS 1:25–29)

THE SEDUCTION OF SIN

Most sin is not seductive at all because it offers no satisfaction. Most human sinning is the product of hatred, envy, boredom, indifference, cowardice, and impotence. In short, most sin gives no pleasure. It is only easier to be a coward than to be brave, easier to be enraged and envious than to be open-hearted and self-satisfied. Such sin is clearly dysfunctional behavior, perverse and ultimately self-destructive.

But what of the sins that promise pleasure? Surely the reluctant Christian will hesitate to follow Jesus if it means giving up the pleasures of life.

Remember St. Paul's simple formula for Christian behavior: Love God and do what you will. What will I miss out on if I follow this formula? Nothing. The Christian enjoys what everyone else enjoys with this distinction: he does not indulge himself, because self-indulgence leads to overindulgence and distraction from God. Then what started out to be pleasant becomes painful. This is the meaning of the Christian's petition in The Lord's Prayer: "Lead us not into temptation." When the monk voluntarily fasts, it is only to discipline himself, not to denigrate the pleasures of eating and drinking. The Amish Christians fashion for themselves a simple life that would not satisfy most of us, but their splendid cooking is a tribute to the pleasures of the palate.

Jesus cautioned against wealth as a distraction, but he in no sense forbade wealth or what money could buy. When we think of "sins of the flesh" we typically mean overindulgence: gluttony, drunkenness, gambling to serious loss. In each case nature takes its revenge: what began as pleasure ends as pain. Drugs are a special case. They offer pleasure but *inevitably* result in pain. Again, the pleasure is not sinful but the predictable consequences are.

SEX: A SPECIAL CASE

Sex is another special case and deserving of more attention. Unique among life's pleasures sex is indulged in private; hence it carries a sense of mystery about it. It is unruly and unpredictable. Hunger and thirst can be satisfied easily and simply, but sexual passion can smolder without any outlet at hand—the reason being that it demands the compliance of another person. The basic function of sex is obvious—procreation—and its intense pleasure attracts us to this extraordinary function that literally creates other human beings.

Sex is a perennial subject for comedy because it makes people act so foolishly. But Christians also realize that—foolish or not—sex is the means by which we cooperate with God in the act of creation. That does not mean we need to be solemn about sex, but we need to acknowledge that among life's pleasures it has by far the most serious consequences and is open to a bewildering variety of perversities and degradations.

Catholic Christians and many fundamentalists believe that the introduction of contraception into sexual relations is sinful because it voids the fundamental purpose of sex. They argue that deliberately separating the pleasure of sex from procreation is akin to a hungry person vomiting a meal so he can enjoy his food and satisfy his hunger without gaining weight. Other Christians argue that since procreation is not the result of every sex act (whereas every meal nourishes), birth control can be employed as responsible behavior.

But most Christians are uneasy about other consequences of separating sex from its function in creation. Masturbation, adultery, homosexuality, sadomasochism, and abortion are clearly uses of sex that pervert its natural purpose and can have other abusive consequences. A permissive society argues that private behavior is one's own personal business. But we know better; private behavior has public consequences. Adultery leads to divorce. Gay lifestyles helped spread the AIDS epidemic. Fetuses are being aborted because they are not the gender desired by the parents. Strictly speaking, sex is not private behavior because it involves two persons. The persistence of pornography throughout history testifies to the weirdness of sexual desire. Imagine a hungry man being satisfied just looking at a meal!

Ideally, sex is the physical expression of romantic love, but even in marriage it is often abused as a way of acting out anger and aggression. Rape, we are told, does not even have pleasure as its motive, but rage instead. Sex is used to degrade and humiliate. Accordingly, let the reluctant Christian take note that while pleasure is good, the pursuit of pleasure often ends in perversity and pain.

LIVING IN LOVE

For all his faults, the Christian does not dwell on either sin or virtue. He accepts Jesus' invitation to follow him, and he follows St. Paul's simple formula, "Love and do what you will," confident that he is responding in kind to a loving God. No one said it better than Paul himself in 1 Corinthians 13:

> If I speak in the tongues of men and of angels, but have not love, I am a noisy gong or a clanging cymbal. And if I have prophetic powers, and understand all mysteries and all knowledge, and if I have all faith, so as to remove mountains, but have not love, I am nothing. If I give away all I have, and if I deliver my body to be burned, but have not love, I gain nothing.
>
> Love is patient and kind; love is not jealous or boastful; it is not arrogant or rude. Love does not insist on its own way; it is not irritable or resentful; it does not rejoice at wrong, but rejoices in the right. Love bears all things, believes all things, hopes all things, endures all things.
>
> Love never ends; as for prophecies, they will pass away; as for tongues, they will

cease; as for knowledge, it will pass away.
For our knowledge is imperfect and our
prophecy is imperfect; but when the perfect
comes, the imperfect will pass away. When I
was a child, I spoke like a child, I thought
like a child, I reasoned like a child; when
I became a man, I gave up childish ways. For
now we see a mirror dimly, but then face to
face. Now I know in part; then I shall
understand fully, even as I have been fully
understood. So faith, hope, love abide, these
three; but the greatest of these is love.

(1 CORINTHIANS 13:1–13)

Jesus' command to love will never satisfy our demand to
know just how to act as a Christian in every instance. Shall
I give money to every homeless person I meet? Do I feed
him? Find him a bed? Take him into my home? The answer
will be different for each Christian. What we must guard
against is minimalism—seeking the least we can get away
with. That is clearly not the way of love but only of
obligation. Sometimes in situations of moral need the
Christian can do nothing but pray.

POSTSCRIPT: HOW GOOD IS GOD?

I began this chapter on morality with Jesus' insistence that "only God is good" and have attempted to show that whoever accepts Jesus' invitation to follow him will discover that love conquers evil. But there are many persons who are not so certain God is good, or who question whether God is good enough to be effective. Rabbi Harold Kushner expressed the problem in the title of his book, *When Bad Things Happen to Good People.* Experience shows that human goodness is not necessarily rewarded, and that innocence is no safeguard against life's cruelties. If God is faithful, why does he not protect us from evil?

The answer is not completely satisfying, but neither are the alternatives of denying God's existence or characterizing him as uncaring or impotent. People tend to define evil as anything that hurts us or someone we love without regard to its source. In short, we locate evil in the pain we feel.

Morality is important, because it keeps people from causing pain to themselves and to one another. But much of the pain in the world cannot be traced to good or bad behavior. If everyone in the world were saintlike there would still be death, disease, and disaster. Moreover, there would still be accidents that result in pain and loss. Does that mean that nature itself is evil or that God diabolically directs his creation in such a way that it causes pain? Clearly not.

Through science, technology, and medicine we seek to avoid being victims of nature. We live longer and more pain-free lives than previous generations. Nations respond to natural disasters with humanitarian assistance. Yet life remains unpredictable and cruel. Why doesn't a good God do something about it?

Jesus' own behavior in his brief public life offers a clue. People clamored for miracles from him: feed us, heal us, restore life, calm the wind and the waves. While Jesus responded generously, he did not pretend to be a constant benefactor making everything right. He employed his miracles to attract attention to what he had to say. Jesus pointed to providence—meaning that God provides— but he did not promise that God would hold nature's reins so tightly that no one could be hurt. Providence does not mean God's dictatorship over every aspect of life. Jesus referred to the lilies of the field and to the sparrows in flight. They are God's creatures, therefore God sustains them. But in the course of nature lilies wither and sparrows die. So too in the course of life we suffer and die.

Jesus said, however, that we are worth "more than many sparrows." To those who follow him, motivated by love, he offers an eternity with God that cannot be compared to all the inequities and iniquities of this life.

QUESTIONS FOR DISCUSSION AND SELF-STUDY:

1. What distinguishes Christians from responsible nonbelievers?

2. Why is evil attractive?

3. What does Jesus mean when he says "Follow me"?

4. Are Jesus' expectations of us realistic?

5. What does St. Paul mean when he refers to the cross as Christ's folly and our following Jesus as foolishness?

CHAPTER 6

WORSHIP AND PRAYER

Ingrained in the heart of every man, woman, and child is the impulse of reverence. At times reverence overrules even the instinct for self-preservation. History is riddled with examples of men and women who have died for devotion—to family, to nation, to principle, or for love of God.

Reverence is the wellspring of religion. For the child it begins as a confused sense of wonder and awe. Primitive religion displays this childish reverence for the awesome, unpredictable power behind the natural world. Even the most sophisticated and skeptical man or woman cannot deny the feeling of awe in mere existence or the feeling of wonder when another human being reaches out and summons his or her love. Love demands devotion which is a kind of reverence made personal.

IDOLATRY

Without direction for their awe and devotion, ancient peoples literally fashioned gods for themselves out of stone and precious metals. In our own times a thwarted, misguided religious impulse led to the worship of the state in Nazi Germany and to the self-sacrificing devotion of individuals to mass revolutions in China and the rest of the communist world.

When the true object of the religious impulse is denied, the impulse itself will not die or go away. Instead, it will turn outward to idolatry of rock stars and politicians, or it will turn in on itself, fostering a generation that pursues its own self-indulgence. The very restlessness that makes us seek God can, if denied, erupt into violence and self-destruction.

Fortunately, God does not hide from mankind. He revealed himself to the Jews and then to his church as the only satisfactory object of reverence. Since the time of Jesus, it has been within the church that we find the setting for the applied reverence we know as worship. Although man can surely pray alone, God clearly asks that we worship together. He first chose the nation of Israel to be his people and to serve him collectively as the People of God. Jesus then expanded the People of God to embrace all who believed in him and who accepted his Father's love. Although Jesus confronted individuals to call forth their faith in him, he founded his church so that Christians might minister to one another in love: "Wherever two or three of you are gather together in my name, I am there in your midst," Jesus promised. And the only prayer he gave his church was one meant to be said not as individuals but together.

THE LORD'S PRAYER

We say not "My Father" but *"Our Father"* following Jesus' lead. And we continue to pray together: "Give us our daily bread; forgive us our trespasses, as we forgive; and lead us not into temptation." In the church, no one is alone. Christ ministers to us in his church; we minister to one another in love; and collectively we call out to God not for his favor to one or another, but for his salvation of us all. Jesus during his lifetime offered an example of worship when he taught in the synagogues and prayed in common with his fellow Israelites. But it was on the night before his death, at his Last Supper, that Jesus dramatized specifically how his followers should worship together. Sharing the same table with his closest companions, the apostles, Jesus made an example of the occasion and the closeness they felt. Taking the food and drink, Jesus thanked God his Father for these gifts. Then, identifying himself with the bread and wine, Jesus shared these simple, life-sustaining gifts with the apostles. "Do this," he told his friends, "to remember me." As a consequence, Jesus' Last Supper became the first thanksgiving feast—a ritual reenacted in some form ever since by nearly every Christian denomination, continuing Christ's sharing of himself with his people.

The reenactment of the Last Supper, known as the Eucharist, is only the most important of many rites of worship in the church.

RITUAL

Worship finds its best expression in ritual. The dignity and importance of man's relationship to God in the church is underlined by the ritual repetition of virtually the same words and actions day after day, Sabbath after Sabbath, century after century. It is a dramatization of eternity. There is nothing necessarily superstitious about ritual, nor is it boring. It is as natural as the rising and setting of the sun and it reflects the common, continuing needs of all peoples. If worship required spontaneity, it would soon become eccentric and frivolous. In everyday life, people require the reassurance of ritual—in graduation ceremonies, wedding rings, the reading of a will. Ritual repetition does not mean hocus-pocus; it is only a sign of seriousness.

Following Jesus' death and Resurrection, his followers continued to share meals with one another in his name in their homes. As time passed and congregations grew

larger, churches were built to accommodate greater numbers and the table of the Last Supper became an altar.
Other important rites were added to surround and dramatize the critical stages in a Christian's life: Baptism and
Confirmation to celebrate birth and growth into the
church; Penance and the Anointing of the Sick to reconcile sinners with their Savior; Matrimony and Ordination
to confirm a life's dedication to husband or wife, or to
service in the church.

THE CHRISTIAN YEAR

Each year the church celebrates anew the major events in
the life of Christ and in its own early life. The church year
begins in late fall with Advent, a month-long period of
preparation for Christmas, during which the church re-
members the history of God's revelation to Israel leading
to the advent of the Savior. Christmas is the church's
celebration of God becoming man in Jesus, born into the
world and fully taking on the joys and sorrows of the life of
his own creatures. Subsequent Sundays trace the growth
of Jesus from infancy through boyhood into maturity,
entering the ministry that would end in death and Resurrection.

In late winter, the church enters the season of Lent, a
period of forty days that has a dual symbolism: first, the
forty years of wandering in the desert that were necessary

before the Jews entered the Promised Land of Israel after enslavement in Egypt; and second, the forty days and nights Jesus himself spent alone in the desert strengthening himself before he began his ministry of teaching, feeding, pardoning, and healing that would end with his execution on the cross.

For Catholic Christians, Lent begins with a reminder that their lives, like that of their Savior, will lead inexorably to death. Ashes are rubbed on their forehead in the shape of a cross, and they are reminded that they were made from dust and will return to dust. With Palm Sunday, the church enters the week it calls Holy, paralleling the last week of Jesus' own life. In many churches palms recall the olive branches that crowds spread before Jesus two thousand years ago as he entered Jerusalem in apparent triumph. On Thursday of Holy Week, the church celebrates the Last Supper, when Christ shared himself as food among his friends. On Good Friday, churches are stripped bare in sorrow as Christians recall their Savior's death on the cross. Easter traditionally begins at midnight with the lighting of a candle in the darkened church. Christ is the light in the darkness, coming back to life. Soon the flame from the single candle symbolizing Christ is shared with a thousand candles held by the faithful, bathing the church in light. Other Christians choose the symbolism of sunrise as they gather at dawn to celebrate the risen Christ.

The triumph of light

Easter is the greatest feast in the church's year-long calendar because it celebrates the triumph of light over darkness, of life over death. It is God's promise fulfilled in Jesus, that life will prevail for those who believe and love. Later, in summer and early autumn, the church recalls Jesus' final sojourn with his friends before returning to his Father. And at Pentecost the church celebrates its own birth, when God's Holy Spirit inspired the apostles to carry on Christ's work and baptize the whole world, making mankind heir to God's promise.

Prayer in the church expresses both the needs of mankind and the grandeur of God. It is common for collective prayer to conclude with the words "through Christ our Lord," dramatizing the role that Jesus, the God-man, plays in reconciling the faithful with the Creator. In the earliest centuries of the church's life it became common for Christians to wake in the middle of the night to pray. Prayer was power against the darkness of a cruel, pagan world and it invited the light of day, symbolizing the Risen Lord. In time a daily schedule of prayer evolved for light and dark hours, whereby Christians—alone or together—could remind themselves of their reliance on God. Prayer became a function of every other element in daily living. Prayer accompanied work. A prayer of thanksgiving preceded each meal.

From the church's infancy, Christians favored a treasury of prayers that had been inspired by King David, founder of the Jewish kingdom a thousand years before Christ. These are the Psalms, a collection of 150 songs expressing the whole range of mankind's emotions as he called out to his God. The original music to the songs has been lost but new settings were composed; at times the Psalms were chanted as simple unrhymed verse. In the words of Jesus' forebear, King David, the Christian could express sorrow and joy, distress and thanksgiving in the Psalms. He could proclaim God's majesty and his love.

COMMON PRAYER

When the monastic movement began to draw numbers of Christians to a common life devoted to work and contemplation, a daily pattern of eight periods of prayer evolved to punctuate their lives. These prayer periods, called "hours," consisted of lessons from the Bible and the common chanting of the Psalms. This regimen dramatized the events of the church year and, in time, became the official prayer or Divine Office, followed not only in the monastery, but by clergy and lay Christians in everyday life in the world.

Prayer is the church's heartbeat. For the Christian, prayer is much more than asking for favors. It is the praise of God's glory, of gratitude for the grandeur of creation, and of sorrow for sin. Common prayer acknowledges that Jesus died to save all people and that he is Lord not of a few but of all, whether believers or not. God loves humanity as a family; as an extended family Christians worship God.

BEYOND MAGIC

Before religion, mankind practiced magic. Magic is the attempt to manipulate the powers behind creation—to trick a fickle God into giving us our way. Religion, by contrast, thinks better of God. Unlike magic, religion is based on respect for the Creator. Rather than trying to cajole God, religion acknowledges that God already has our best interests at heart. Religious living is the faithful attempt to cooperate with him.

In attempting to shrug off any lingering resemblances to magic, however, religions run the risk of obscurity. Without ritual and grounding in material life, religion can become too spiritual and unworldly for mankind's own good. Man is created as something less than the angels. He has a mind and a spirit, both of which he can lift up to God. But day in and day out he is still only a sophisticated animal in a material world. He must operate by his senses of sight and hearing, of touch, taste, and smell. He is subject to the heat and the cold, to hunger and thirst, to pain and death. Any religion that treats man as if he had only a mind and a soul is a faith that falsifies mankind. Moreover, a strictly "spiritual" religion denigrates God's own creation of a physical world.

God dramatized this message himself when he sent his own Son to become man—as fully and physically human as any man or woman who ever lived. During his ministry on earth, Jesus communicated with people through their senses—touching them, feeding them, healing them, and speaking to them. Even after his death and Resurrection, when Jesus rejoined his Father, he was not a disembodied spirit, but fully human. The message is clear: God's creation is good. It is good to be alive and good to be flesh-and-blood men and women. God saves whole persons, not just souls.

Accordingly, in its role of perpetuating the saving presence of Jesus among his people, the church acts as Jesus did, teaching, healing, blessing, feeding, and forgiving real persons in real life. Evangelical Christian communities still hold rites to heal the minds and bodies of their suffering members, seeking to continue in our own time the healing ministry of Jesus. From the earliest centuries, the church has sought to institutionalize Jesus' concern for the health of body as well as soul. This explains why there are still so many Christian hospitals and nursing homes serving communities throughout the world. The Christian medical missionary was common in the age of colonization and is still a fixture in the Third World.

Catholic Christians exemplify how, through its rites, the church continues to apply Jesus' ministry to the faithful. But all Christian denominations provide some sacramental vehicles for Jesus' presence and saving work. Catholic church buildings are treasure houses of sacramentality, from holy water and incense to palms, oils, and stained-glass windows that illustrate stories from the Bible. Admittedly, many of these symbols are not of crucial importance; what is important is the consistent way the church through material things insists on Christ's active presence in God's creation.

Of course, there is always a danger of superstition and idolatry—of pretending that a symbol or rite has a magical power of its own apart from Jesus. For many centuries, Christians convinced themselves that relics—bones and possessions of the saints—possessed such power. Today all Christians avoid such superstition, but all equally reject a disembodied Christianity that consists of only pious feelings, passive meditation, and moral aspirations.

SACRAMENTS

The original meaning of the word "sacrament" is a pledge of allegiance. The sacrament of Christian initiation—Baptism—retains some of that original sense of personal commitment. But in the Scriptures the word "sacrament" refers more broadly to the mysterious reality of God's activity on behalf of mankind as revealed in his Son, Jesus. Therefore, anything or any person or any event that serves to connect men or women with God's saving love can be called, loosely, a sacrament.

Jesus himself was born into a Jewish world that was, in this sense, richly sacramental. The Old Testament reminds us that the Jews were constantly made aware of God's presence through ritual meals and sacrifices, kisses and blessings, oils and washings. From the time of King Solomon, nine hundred years before Christ, the Jews practiced an official confession of sins. And Jewish rabbis anointed the sick with oil. Jesus fully entered into a sacramental world, accepting Baptism by his cousin John at the River Jordan and an anointing by Mary Magdalene before his death. The church developed many of these Jewish rituals and added others, seven of which Catholic Christians consider most important because they represent Jesus' major initiatives. These seven most important and authentic rites are what they now mean by the "sacraments."

There is nothing especially significant about the number of the sacraments. Jesus himself, strictly speaking, is the only real "sacrament" because he is the connection between God and man. But these seven rites are the seven most important ways in which Jesus continues to work in his church. The seven rites are Baptism, Penance, the Eucharist, Confirmation, Matrimony, Holy Orders, and the Anointing of the Sick.

Baptism is initiation into the church—Jesus reaching through his church to call men, women, and children to accept God's love and salvation. Penance is Jesus acting through his church to forgive the Christian who repents of his sins and resolves to live a life of integrity. The Eucharist is Jesus sharing himself again with his friends through the church in a memorial of the Last Supper he shared with his apostles. It is also known as Communion. Catholics call its celebration the Mass. Confirmation is Jesus confirming the adult commitment of his followers. Since many Christians are baptized in infancy, a faith commitment awaits maturity—at least pre-adolescence.

OTHER RITES

Matrimony is Jesus raising human love to approach the love God bears for his church, and Jesus joining the Creator with the human act of regeneration. This is a sacrament actually performed by husband and wife. The church is but the witness to their vows. Holy Orders or ordination is Jesus calling through his church to select Christians as he did his apostles—"Follow me"—to minister to his church. This is why ministry is known as a "calling." Anointing is Jesus in his church continuing to console the sick and dying, just as he did when he walked among men and women in Israel. Miracles are not to be expected, but even when bodies remain sick, the spirits of the anointed are often revitalized.

Over time rituals become habitual and often mindless and superstitious. Much of the revolt of Protestant Christianity was against ritual emptied of meaning. In our own time the revived sense of mystery and encounter in ritual is based on a deeper understanding of how God acts. This involves a sensitive reading of both the Jewish and Christian Scriptures to determine how God has acted in the past and how he intends the church to continue his work.

GRACE

God's intentions are consistent; his saving actions recur from generation to generation. Ritual celebrates God's past and still continuing initiatives to meet mankind's recurring needs. The form of ritual is important because it must foster the sense of real encounter between man and his God. Every birth, every meal, and every death is outwardly like every other, yet a unique experience for each individual. The sacramental encounter of God in his church must draw the individual Christian from his isolation into the family of man and into the love of God. Therefore, rites and worship are properly communal activities, dramatizing not only God's concern for the individual, but his command that they love one another.

The effect of the sacramental encounter is known as grace. The encounter itself "graces" the Christian and there is no way to refer to a relationship as conferring more or less grace. It is either intimate or distant. What is critical is that the Christian be moved by the symbols of the sacrament to understand his needs and open himself to God's action. For this reason the rites of the sacraments

will continue to change in order to elicit the intellectual
and emotional recognition that God is meeting the Christian in the here and now, not in some storybook-like
quaint past. The sacraments must evoke that sense of awe
and wonder the first man and woman felt at the immensity
of creation and the mystery of being alive.

SPIRITUALITY

During his life on earth Jesus resisted praise: "Why do you
call me good? Only God is good." But in the same breath,
he made immense demands upon his followers: "Be perfect, as your heavenly Father is perfect," he insisted. Christian life rests on a paradox that only God is good yet the
Christian must seek the perfection that properly belongs
to God. Jesus himself resolved the paradox by his utter
obedience to God's will. It is God's own goodness that
perfects mankind.

The purpose of our lives, therefore, is for us to become
so responsive to God that we are filled by him. Only God
is good, but every man, woman, and child can be filled to
overflowing with that goodness. Were it not for the example of Jesus himself, this would be only a theory or pious
hope. Fortunately, every Christian has the model of Christ
himself to follow. Christian life is the imitation of Christ.
Goodness is not simply a slavish adherence to codes of
ethical behavior. The Pharisees put Jesus to death pre-

cisely because he exposed their righteousness as hypocrisy. He proved by breaking rules that God and goodness are not served by formulas.

Jesus' preference for the company of sinners, moreover, suggests that we must identify goodness as something distinct from sinlessness. All Christians, no matter how "good" they are deemed, must rightly consider themselves sinners. They are saved, of course, but sinners nonetheless. We do not "save" ourselves. Sin is alienation: a choice of self over God. Jesus appealed to sinners who were ripe for the life he had to offer and had no illusions about the loneliness of sin.

The other clue to the meaning of goodness comes from the word "good," so like the word "God." Goodness is God-likeness. It is intimacy with God—the God-life overflowing into human life. St. John declares, "God is love." But love is not sufficient unto itself; it begs for union with another. In God that union of love is called the Trinity. But God calls to mankind as well. As the creature came from God, it rightly finds its home in him. Alone among all God's creatures, men and women were adopted by him. God himself became human to dramatize the intimacy he intends.

The purpose of life is totally centered on God, in this life as well as the next. This "serving" of God comes closest to the everyday definition of goodness. But service is only part of what life is about; it is also about knowing God and loving him as well.

KNOWING AND LOVING

Knowing and loving God are responsibilities on the same order as breathing and eating—totally natural, continuous, and lifegiving. What is more-than-natural is God's gift of such knowledge. Children ask, "What will it be like in heaven?" Adults no longer raise the question or they picture the next life as a remedy for this one; a relief from care, conflict, and suffering. But the next life is more properly an extension, or more accurately, a fulfillment of this one. The spiritual life consists of the conscious and deliberate attempt by the Christian to know and love God now—in *this* life.

To embark upon a spiritual life is wholly positive and practical: positive, because it looks to God for fulfillment, not relief, and practical because the spiritual life holds that since heaven is marriage with God, it is sensible to begin the engagement in this life. Pride, pleasure, ambition, and power are subordinated by the serious Christian not because they are evil, but because they are distracting and ultimately pointless. "What does it profit a man if he gains the whole world?" Jesus demands, knowing that only God can satisfy mankind. Since "our hearts are restless until they rest in thee," all else—good, bad, or indifferent—distracts from life's purpose.

The spiritual life is not irresponsible, but it is simple, because it has a single objective—God—and a single motive—love. Therefore, a serious Christian seeks to un-complicate his life. However, he cannot shrug off duty. Since every Christian has the duty of loving his or her fellowman as well as loving God, he or she cannot escape life's responsibilities. A Christian must keep his feet planted firmly on the ground though his heart and head are in the air. While spirituality is ultimately simple, it is, in practice, difficult. We do not grasp God with our physical senses. He is not visible to our eyes, nor does he speak private words in our ears. Christians must proceed by faith and hope and love—not totally in the dark, but in the dusk, when outlines and objects are unclear. God gives us the grace to proceed. He is not the end of our search—not some lost Grail at the end of a pilgrimage. Rather, his Holy Spirit dwells within us on the journey. Paradoxically, although we travel to God, we have already arrived. Although we search for God, he has already found us.

Chief among God's graces in the spiritual life is his church. The church exists precisely as a medium for encountering Christ with our fellow Christians in the Scriptures and the sacraments. All members of the church are, consequently, graces to one another, sharing their individual love and knowledge for mutual benefit. The church, far from being an obstacle to individual freedom to seek God, is itself God's gift of "the way, the truth, and the life."

FAITH, HOPE, LOVE

"The just man lives by faith." If the purpose of life is to know God, then faith is the only doorway. Faith is not knowledge but offers access to it. As St. Paul says, only later will we "see God face to face." Faith means saying yes to God's revelation. It is accepting God's point of view rather than our own. Faith is not simply passive acceptance of a vast array of religious information. To see with the eyes of faith is to see life whole and at once with the eyes of God himself.

Faith is not completely satisfying. It is not certainty. It often coexists with painful, agonizing doubt. But the alternative is worse: to see life through our eyes alone. Jesus himself was tempted by doubt. On the cross he cried out his apparent abandonment by his Father: "Why have you forsaken me?" But faith overcomes doubt: "Not my will, but yours be done." Although faith lacks complete evidence, it is in no way unreasonable. Faith never rests content with itself. It is not self-assured. Rather, faith constantly seeks understanding and confirmation. The spiritual Christian cries out to Jesus in the voice of the man in the Gospels: "I believe; help my unbelief." On this evidence of faith tested by doubt, Jesus healed the man's son.

Hope joins faith with love as one of the three God-centered virtues of the spiritual life. Hope is not naive and sunny; it is realistic and patient. The faithful Christian has a hope rooted in the assurance that God is adequate to his needs and the needs of the world—that tragedies, however poignant, are not the final chapters. Although God is known only imperfectly through faith, our love for God confirms that knowledge. A lover's knowledge is preferable to a scientist's because it produces a bond rather than an insight. Love is the first and complete commandment: "You shall love the Lord your God with all your heart, and with all your soul, and with all your mind."

God does not need to be loved. Within his own Trinity he *is* love. Mankind, however, needs to be loved by God, since we are insufficient unto ourselves and can be completed only by the Maker who knows our pattern. For us love is the abandonment of a selfish, closed autonomy. Love is not our creation, but God's. In a spiritual life the dedicated Christian does not try to summon love for God; rather, he allows God's spirit within him to expand and possess him.

All who have lived deeply can appreciate the value and the demands of love. Every human being feels inadequate as a solitary individual yet is frightened of the loving surrender to another that is the cost of ending that isolation. God, the divine lover, lacks the physical immediacy of a human loved one. But he alone can satisfy the longing of the heart for he is not only the creator of love but love itself.

PRAYER

A spiritual life is a life of prayer. In the early Christian church, households rose at midnight to sing songs of expectation for the return of Jesus. The best prayers are the collective prayers of the church—the prayers that begin with the word "We." The loving community is an impetus to love the Lord. From antiquity the church has prescribed a day-long Divine Office, the liturgical "hours," consisting largely of the Psalms of David, sung or chanted in common at intervals from the rising to the setting of the sun.

Prayer is conversation with God. As far as mere words go, prayer is admittedly one-sided. But it is not frustrating. God's Spirit, dwelling with the Christian, prays with us if we let him. Prayer is not only useful, it is a foretaste of eternity when man and God will communicate face-to-face in love. God is approachable in prayer through Christ who, although he is God's son, was made human like ourselves. With Jesus we can pray to "Our Father."

Prayer is not detached from life. As Jesus warned, "Not everyone who says to me, 'Lord, Lord' shall enter into the kingdom of heaven, but he who does the will of my Father." The God to whom the Christian prays is not isolated in some heaven apart; he is the God whose Son died for this world and whose Holy Spirit abides here. A responsible, loving life is not only the medium of prayer but the substance of it.

Those who progress in prayer set time aside for meditation, no longer actively speaking to God, but quietly pondering the richness of what God has revealed or given. Some Christians have so opened themselves to God in prayer that he is able to break through the ordinary barriers of consciousness and reveal himself directly. The saints who have attempted to explain these brief, direct encounters with God invariably fail because they must rely on words describing ordinary human experience. God cannot be captured in words. In recent years larger numbers of Christians claim to have received direct inspiration from the Holy Spirit, reminiscent of the gifts of prophecy in the primitive church. But God requires the same thing of them as he does of the rest of us.

Although there are no shortcuts to the knowledge and love of God, the primitive church upheld poverty, chastity, and obedience as conditions of life favorable to spirituality. However, a solitary or monastic lifestyle is not virtuous unless it focuses attention totally on God. Any dedicated life involves a simplifying and emptying of the attachments that can distract from the object of our lives. Whatever one's station in life, each Christian is a son or daughter of God, summoned to an eternity of intimacy with him: "No eye has seen, nor ear heard, nor the heart of man conceived what God has prepared for those who love him."

PRAYER: ASKING FOR THE
RIGHT THINGS

In principle prayer consists of conversation between ourselves and God. In practice we do the talking, God the
listening. What kind of conversation is that? It's similar to
the communications we have with a doctor or lawyer or
repairman: "Here's my problem, fix it, will you?"

Prayer is not chit-chat between equals. We do not want
to know God's problems (*we* are his problems, and only he
can set us right). Think of the times you have been immo-
bilized by dentist or hairdresser and had to listen to their
inane monologues; let us not bore God with gossip and
trivia!

Doctors, lawyers, psychiatrists, and repairmen don't say
much. Their silence means they're paying attention to us.
So with God. But we must get to the point if we're to be
helped. (I think of my mechanic's exasperation as I try to
explain my sick car's symptoms when I haven't the foggiest
notion what's under the hood.)

Learning to pray well consists of learning to explain to
God more accurately what ails us so that he can help.
Praying well means respecting God as our Savior (our
repairman, if you will). No doctor can assist a patient who
refuses to care for himself. Learning to pray well means
taking our medicine—allowing God to help, not miraculously, but by restoring us to the kind of creature he had in
mind when he created our race. When you learn to pray

well and often you will no longer wait to break down before seeking God's help; you will be practicing a kind of preventive medicine.

Be assured, prayer is a lopsided conversation between unequal partners. We ask God for help; he doesn't need ours. Similarly he's not about to thank us, or praise us, or seek our forgiveness. We're the ones to put praise, gratitude, and repentance into our side of the conversation.

At the end of this chapter there are several examples of prayers that have stood the test of time. You will find expressed in them some sentiments that will help you pray effectively. The first lesson is that we probably don't know what we need from God. Oscar Wilde and George Bernard Shaw hit it right—if we use prayer as wish-fulfillment, we are courting disaster.

To start praying, let us go to God as we would to a doctor or repairman with what ails us but without presuming we know the cure. Do this daily either first thing in the morning or late in the day when you have a few quiet, uninterrupted minutes. Do it aloud or silently, standing, sitting, or kneeling. Below is a sample with some direction in the right column:

Address God personally: *Accept responsibility:*	God, I know I'm responsible for myself, but I'm not handling some things very well. I don't always try hard enough, but even when I do

Admit you don't have all the answers:

Admit you may not even know the real problem:

Acknowledge Jesus' sacrifice of love:

Think of your effect on others:

Ask God to solve your problem his way:

Accept final responsibility:

I'm not sure what's most important. Here's what I think my problem is (explain in your own words). But you know better. If I were a more faithful person I wouldn't get into some of these fixes and I wouldn't be so confused. Forgive me for not being the person you created me to be and sent your Son Jesus to die for. And forgive me for creating problems for other people as I try to take care of myself. God, I admit I may be praying for the wrong thing. But you know what I need and what I must do. Give me the courage to face the truth and strength to change. Help me, God, to stop being part of the problem and to start being part of the solution.

P.S.: Since you're talking to yourself all day long, why not make God a party to your thoughts? Calling upon his presence is praying, whether you talk or not. Asking God to be part of your thoughts can transform your daydreaming into something that just might change your life.

PRAYERS FOR PERSONAL USE

Christianity teaches that the purpose of life is to see God—to overcome the isolation from our source of being and alienation from our true selves that compromises all we have. The life of prayer is an anticipation of the closeness to God that will mark the successful conclusion of our earthly lives. Prayer is practice for the real thing: face to face communication with God.

Some Christians, notably monks, get a jump on eternity by devoting themselves to prayer as a way of life this side of the grave. Assuming that you are not a candidate for the monastery, it nevertheless makes sense to cultivate the sense of God's presence, to speak with him, to share with him, and to let him fill your silences.

Here is a brief treasury of prayers to get you started. Just as few of us are poets but must purchase greeting cards to express our sentiments, most of us do well to borrow from those who have greater facility with prayer. Don't be intimidated by these prayers; use them as starters but speak to God from your own heart. I hope these examples help you.

PRAYERS OF JESUS

Our Father who art in heaven,
Hallowed be thy name.
Thy kingdom come,
Thy will be done,
On earth as it is in heaven.
Give us this day our daily bread;
And forgive us our debts,
As we also have forgiven our debtors;
And lead us not into temptation,
But deliver us from evil.

(MATTHEW 6: 6-13)

I thank thee, Father, Lord of heaven and earth, that
thou has hidden these things from the wise and
understanding and revealed them to babes; yea,
Father, for such was thy gracious will. All things
have been delivered to me by my Father; and no
one knows who the Son is except the Father, or
who the Father is except the Son and anyone to
whom the Son chooses to reveal him.

(LUKE 10: b-22)

Father, I thank thee that thou hast heard me. I knew that thou hearest me always, but I have said this on account of the people standing by, that they may believe that thou didst send me.

(JOHN 11: 41b-42)

Father, forgive them; for they know not what they do.

(LUKE 23: 34)

Father, into thy hands I commit my spirit!

(LUKE 23: 46)

OTHER PRAYERS FROM SCRIPTURE

The Lord is my shepherd: therefore can I lack
    nothing.
He shall feed me in a green pasture: and lead me
    forth beside the waters of comfort.
He shall convert my soul: and bring me forth in the
    paths of righteousness, for his Name's sake.
Yea, though I walk through the valley of the
    shadow of death, I will fear no evil: for thou art
    with me: thy rod and thy staff comfort me.
Thou shalt prepare a table before me against them

that trouble me: thou hast anointed my head
with oil, and my cup shall be full.
But thy loving-kindness and mercy shall follow me
all the days of my life: and I will dwell in the
house of the Lord forever.

(PSALM 23)

Nevertheless, though I am sometime afraid: yet put
I my trust in thee.

(PSALM 56: 3)

Lord, I am not worthy that thou shouldest enter
under my roof: but speak the word only, and my
soul shall be healed.

(BASED ON LUKE 7: 6–7)

Lord, what wilt thou have me to do?

(ACTS 22: 10)

PRAYERS OF THE CHURCH

We praise thee, O God: we acknowledge thee to be
the Lord. All the earth doth worship thee the
Father everlasting. To thee all Angels cry aloud
the Heavens, and all the Powers therein.
To thee Cherubim and Seraphim continually do
cry,

Holy, Holy, Holy: Lord God of Sabaoth;
Heaven and earth are full of the Majesty of thy
  Glory.
The glorious company of the Apostles praise thee.
The goodly fellowship of the Prophets praise thee.
The noble army of Martyrs praise thee.
The holy Church throughout all the word doth
  acknowledge thee;
The Father of an infinite Majesty;
Thine honourable, true and only Son;
Also the Holy Ghost the Comforter . . .

TE DEUM LAUDAMUS

Lamb of God, you take away the sins of the world:
  have mercy on us.
Lamb of God, you take away the sins of the world:
  have mercy on us.
Lamb of God, you take away the sins of the world:
  grant us peace.

THE ROMAN MISSAL

O Lord Jesus Christ, who didst say to thine
apostles: Peace I leave with you, my peace I give
unto you; regard not our sins, but the faith of thy
Church, and grant her that peace and unity which
is according to thy will: Who livest and reignest
God, throughout all ages, world without end.

THE ROMAN MISSAL

O Lord, who hast taught us that all our doings
without love are nothing worth; send thy Holy
Spirit, and pour into our hearts that most excellent
gift of love, the very bond of peace and of all
virtues, without which whosoever liveth is counted
dead before thee. Grant this for thine only Son
Jesus Christ's sake.

BOOK OF COMMON PRAYER

Save us, O Lord, while waking, and guard us while
sleeping: that awake we may watch with Christ,
and asleep we may rest in peace.

COMPLINE, SARUM BREVIARY

PRAYERS FOR HELP & INSPIRATION

Dear God, be good to me;
The sea is so wide,
And my boat is so small.

BRETON FISHERMEN'S PRAYER

In me there is darkness,
But with you there is light;
I am lonely, but you do not leave me;
I am feeble in heart, but with you there is help;

I am restless, but with you there is peace.
In me there is bitterness, but with you there is
    patience;
I do not understand your ways,
But you know the way for me . . .

> DIETRICH BONHOEFFER, WRITTEN WHILE
> AWAITING EXECUTION IN A NAZI PRISON

O thou great Chief, light a candle in my heart, that
I may see what is therein, and sweep the rubbish
from thy dwelling place.

> AN AFRICAN SCHOOLGIRL'S PRAYER

I pray thee for thy great mercy and by the token of
    the holy rood,
Guide me to thy will, to my soul's need, better than
    I can myself;
And shield me against my foes, seen and unseen;
And teach me to do thy will
    that I may inwardly love thee before all things
    with a clean mind and a clean body.
For thou art my maker and my redeemer,
    my help, my comfort, my trust, and my hope.
Praise and glory be to thee now, ever and ever,
    world without end.

> KING ALFRED, 849–901

May the strength of God pilot us. May the power
of God preserve us. May the wisdom of God
instruct us. May the hand of God protect us. May
the way of God direct us. May the shield of God
defend us.

ST. PATRICK, 389–461
CELTIC MONK AND EVANGELIST OF IRELAND

O God, you have glorified our victorious Savior
with a visible, triumphant resurrection from the
dead, and ascension into heaven, where he sits
at your right hand; grant, we beg you, that his
triumphs and glories may ever shine in our eyes,
to make us more clearly see through his sufferings,
and more courageously endure our own; being
assured by his example, that if we endeavor to live
and die like him, for the advancement of your love
in ourselves and others, you will raise our dead
bodies again, and conforming them to his glorious
body, call us above the clouds, and give us
possession of your everlasting kingdom.

JOHN WESLEY, 1703–1791
ANGLICAN PRIEST AND INSPIRATION FOR
THE METHODIST CHURCH

PRAYERS OF REPENTANCE & GRATEFULNESS

See, Lord, an empty vessel that needs to be filled. My Lord, fill it. I am weak in the faith; strengthen me. I am cold in love, warm me and make me fervent so that my love may go out to my neighbor. I do not have a strong and firm faith; at times I doubt and am unable to trust you altogether. O Lord, help me. Strengthen my faith and trust in you. In you I have sealed all the treasures I have. I am poor; you are rich and came to be merciful to the poor. I am a sinner; you are upright. With me there is an abundance of sin; in you is the fullness of righteousness. Therefore, I will remain with you from whom I can receive, but to whom I may not give. Amen.

MARTIN LUTHER, 1483–1546
THE GREAT GERMAN REFORMER

Were you there when they crucified my Lord?
   Were you there?
O sometimes it causes me to tremble, tremble,
   tremble,
   Were you there when they crucified my
Lord? . . .

AFRICAN AMERICAN SPIRITUAL

O Lord, remember not only the men and women of good will, but also those of ill will. But do not remember all the suffering they have inflicted on us; remember the fruits we have bought, thanks to this suffering—our comradeship, our loyalty, our humility, our courage, our generosity, the greatness of heart which has grown out of all this, and when they come to judgment let all the fruits which we have borne be their forgiveness.

PRAYER WRITTEN BY AN UNKNOWN PRISONER
IN RAVENSBRUCK CONCENTRATION CAMP AND
LEFT BY THE BODY OF A DEAD CHILD

I asked for strength that I might achieve;
I was made weak that I might learn humbly to obey.
I asked for health that I might do greater things;
I was given infirmity that I might do better things.
I asked for riches that I might be happy;
I was given poverty that I might be wise.
I asked for power that I might have the praise of
    men;
I was given weakness that I might feel the need of
    God.
I asked for all things that I might enjoy life;
I was given life that I might enjoy all things.
I got nothing that I had asked for,
But everything that I had hoped for.

Almost despite myself my unspoken prayers were
   answered;
>   I AM, AMONG ALL MEN, MOST RICHLY BLESSED.

>   PRAYER OF AN UNKNOWN CONFEDERATE SOLDIER

PRAYERS FOR LOVE OF GOD

I am serene because I know thou lovest me.
Because thou lovest me, naught can move me from
   my peace.
Because thou lovest me, I am as one to whom all
   good has come.

>   GAELIC, TR. ALISTAIR MACLEAN

You, O eternal Trinity, are a deep sea, into which
the more I enter the more I find, and the more I
find the more I seek. The soul cannot be satiated in
your abyss, for she continually hungers after you,
the eternal Trinity, desiring to see you with the
light of your light. As the hart desires the springs of
living water, so my soul desires to leave the prison
of this dark body and see you in truth.

>   CATHERINE OF SIENA, 1347–1380
>   DOMINICAN LAYWOMAN AND CONSULTANT
>   TO POPES

Open wide the window of our spirits, O Lord, and
fill us full of light; open wide the door of our
hearts, that we may receive and entertain you with
all our powers of adoration and love.

CHRISTINA ROSSETTI, 1830–1894
ENGLISH POET

O gracious and holy Father,
Give us wisdom to perceive you,
intelligence to understand you,
diligence to seek you,
patience to wait for you,
eyes to see you,
a heart to meditate on you,
and a life to proclaim you,
through the power of the Spirit of Jesus Christ our
    Lord.

ST. BENEDICT, 480–547
FOUNDER OF WESTERN CHRISTIAN MONASTICISM

You are never weary, O Lord, of doing us good. Let
   us never be
weary of serving you. But as you have pleasure in
   the prosperity
of your servants, so let us take pleasure in the
service of our Lord, and abound in your work, and
in your love and praise evermore. O fill up all that
is wanting, reform whatever is amiss in us, perfect
what concerns us, let the witness of our pardoning
love ever abide in all our hearts.

JOHN WESLEY

Not with the hope of gaining aught,
Not seeking a reward;
But as thyself hast loved me,
O ever-loving Lord!
E'en so I love thee, and will love,
And in thy praise will sing,
Solely because thou art my God,
and my eternal King.

LATIN, 17TH CENTURY, TR. E. CASWALL

Godhead here in hiding, whom I do adore
Masked by these bare shadows, shape and nothing
   more,
See, Lord, at thy service low lies here a heart
Lost, all lost in wonder at the God thou art . . .
Jesu whom I look at shrouded here below,
I beseech thee send me what I thirst for so,
Some day to gaze on thee face to face in light
And be blest for ever with thy glory's sight.

> LATIN, 13TH CENTURY,
> TR. GERARD MANLEY HOPKINS, 1844–89

O God within my breast
Almighty ever-present
Life, that in me hast rest
As I Undying Life, have power in Thee.

With wide-embracing love
Thy spirit animates eternal years
Pervades and broods above,
Changes, sustains, dissolves, creates and rears.

Though Earth and moon were gone
And suns and universes ceased to be
And thou wert left alone
Every Existence would exist in thee.

There is not room for Death
Nor atom that his might could render void
Since thou art Being and Breath
And what thou art may never be destroyed.

EMILY BRONTË
ENGLAND, 19TH CENTURY

PRAYERS FOR FAITH & DEDICATION

And now unto him who is able to keep us from
falling and lift us from the dark valley of despair
to the mountains of hope, from the midnight of
desperation to the daybreak of joy; to him be
power and authority, for ever and ever. Amen.

MARTIN LUTHER KING, JR., 1929–1968
AMERICAN CLERGYMAN AND SOCIAL REFORMER

We resign into your hands our sleeping bodies, our cold
hearths and open doors. Give us to awaken with smiles;
give us to labor smiling. As the sun returns in the east,
so let our patience be renewed with dawn; as the sun
lightens the world, so let our loving-kindness brighten
this house of our habitation.

ROBERT LOUIS STEVENSON, 1850–1894
SCOTTISH ESSAYIST, NOVELIST, AND POET

Use me, my Savior, for whatever purpose and in whatever way you may require. Here is my poor heart, an empty vessel: fill it with your grace. Here is my sinful and troubled soul: quicken it and refresh it with your love. Take my heart for your abode; my mouth to spread abroad the glory of your name; my love and all my powers for the advancement of your believing people; and never allow the steadfastness and confidence of my faith to abate.

> DWIGHT L. MOODY, 1837–1899
> AMERICAN EVANGELIST AND EDUCATOR

PRAYERS TO SUMMON THE SPIRIT

O Lord, you who are all merciful, take away my sins from me, and enkindle within me the fire of your Holy Spirit. Take away this heart of stone from me, and give me a heart of flesh and blood, a heart to love and adore you, a heart which may delight in you, love you and please you, for Christ's sake.

> ST. AMBROSE, 339–397
> BISHOP OF MILAN

Because we have need continually to crave many things at your hands, we humbly beg you, O heavenly Father, to grant us your Holy Spirit to direct our petitions, that they may proceed from such a fervent mind as may be agreeable to your holy will. Amen.

JOHN KNOX, 1513–1572
SCOTTISH REFORMER

Enlighten us, O God, by your Spirit, in the understanding of your Word, and grant us the grace to receive it in true fear and humility, that we may learn to put our trust in you, to fear and honor you, by glorifying your Holy Name in all our life, and to yield you the love and obedience which faithful servants owe to their master and children to their fathers, seeing it has led you to call us to the number of your servants and children.

JOHN CALVIN, 1509–1564
FRENCH THEOLOGIAN AND REFORMER IN GENEVA

PRAYERS FOR EVERYDAY LIVING

Make us remember, O God, that every day is your gift, to be used according to your command.

> SAMUEL JOHNSON, 1709–1784
> ENGLISH WRITER AND LEXICOGRAPHER

Lead, kindly Light, amid the encircling gloom,
   Lead Thou me on,
The night is dark and I am far from home,
   Lead Thou me on,
Keep Thou my feet: I do not ask to see
The distant scene; one step's enough for me

> JOHN HENRY NEWMAN, 1801–1890
> CARDINAL, THEOLOGIAN, AND MAN OF LETTERS

O Lord, let nothing divert our advances towards you, but in this dangerous labyrinth of the world and the whole course of our pilgrimage here, your heavenly dictates be our map and your holy life be our guide.

> JOHN WESLEY, 1803–1791
> ANGLICAN PRIEST AND FOUNDER OF
> THE METHODIST CHURCH

Christ, be with me, Christ before me, Christ
  behind me,
Christ in me, Christ beneath me, Christ above me,
Christ on my right, Christ on my left,
Christ where I lie, Christ where I sit, Christ where I
  arise,
Christ in the heart of every one who thinks of me,
Christ in every eye that sees me,
Christ in every ear that hears me.

> ST. PATRICK (389–461)
> CELTIC MONK AND EVANGELIST OF IRELAND

Let not the future trouble thee: thou wilt encounter
it, if need be, with the same sword of reason in thy
hand that now serves thee against the present.

    All things are interwoven each with the other: the
tie is sacred, and nothing, or next to nothing, is alien
to aught else. They are all coordinated to one end,
and all go to form the same universe. For there is one
universe comprising all things, one God pervading
all things, one substance and one law; and there is
one reason common to all intellectual beings, and
one truth; for there is one perfection for all life that
is kindred and shares in the same reason.

> MARCUS AURELIUS
> ROMAN EMPEROR AND STOIC PHILOSOPHER

Guard for me my eyes, Jesus Son of Mary, lest
   seeing another's wealth make me covetous.
Guard for me my ears, lest they hearken to slander,
   lest they listen constantly to folly in the sinful
   world.
Guard for me my heart, O Christ, in thy love, lest I
   ponder wretchedly the desire of any iniquity.
Guard for me my hands, that they be not stretched
   out for quarrelling, that they may not, after that,
   practice shameful supplication.
Guard for me my feet upon the gentle earth of
   Ireland, lest, bent on profitless errands, they
   abandon rest.

           IRISH

Make us worthy, Lord,
To serve our fellowmen
Throughout the world who live and die
in poverty or hunger.

Give them through our hands
This day their daily bread
And by our understanding love
Give peace and joy.

         MOTHER TERESA OF CALCUTTA

O God of earth and altar,
Bow down and hear our cry,
Our earthly rulers falter,
Our people drift and die;
The walls of gold entomb us,
The swords of scorn divide,
Take not your thunder from us,
But take away our pride!

G. K. CHESTERTON, 1874–1936
ENGLISH JOURNALIST AND WRITER

O Lord, you know how busy I must be this day; if I forget you, do not forget me: for Christ's sake.

SIR JACOB ASTLEY, 1579–1652
BEFORE THE BATTLE OF EDGE HILL IN 1642

O Lord, baptize our hearts into a sense of the conditions and needs of all people.

GEORGE FOX, 1624–1691
FOUNDER OF THE SOCIETY OF FRIENDS

O God, help us not to despise what we do not understand.

WILLIAM PENN, 1644–1718
QUAKER LEADER AND FOUNDER
OF PENNSYLVANIA

I have just hung up; why did he telephone?
I don't know . . . Oh! I get it . . .
I talked a lot and listened very little.

Forgive me, Lord, it was a monologue and not a
　dialogue.
I explained my idea and did not get his;
Since I didn't listen, I learned nothing,
Since I didn't listen, I didn't help,
Since I didn't listen, we didn't communicate.

Forgive me, Lord, for we were connected,
and now we are cut off.

　　　MICHAEL QUOIST

Deliver us, good Lord, from the excessive demands
of business and social life that limit family
relationship; from the insensitivity and harshness of
judgment that prevent understanding; from
domineering ways and selfish imposition of our
will; from softness and indulgence mistaken for
love. Bless us with wise and understanding hearts
that we may demand neither too much nor too
little, and grant us such a measure of love that we
may nurture our children to that fullness of

manhood and womanhood, which you purposed for
them, through Jesus Christ our Lord.

> CHARLES S. MARTIN (B. 1906)
> HEADMASTER OF ST. ALBAN'S SCHOOL,
> WASHINGTON, D.C.

Underneath are my bad tyres.
The brakes are unreliable.
Unfortunately I have no money,
and parts are difficult to get.
Lord,
I did not overload the truck.
Lord,
'Jesus is mine'
is written on the vehicle,
for without him I would not drive
a single mile.
The people in the back are relying on me.
They trust me because they see the words:
'Jesus is mine.'
Lord,
I trust you!

> TRUCK DRIVER'S PRAYER
> BY A YOUNG GHANIAN CHRISTIAN

Lord, make me an instrument of your peace. Where there is hatred, let me sow love; where there is injury, pardon; where there is doubt, faith; where there is despair, hope; where there is darkness, light; where there is sadness, joy.

O divine Master, grant that I may not so much seek to be consoled, as to console; to be understood, as to understand; to be loved, as to love. For it is in giving that we receive; it is in pardoning that we are pardoned; and it is in dying that we are born to eternal life.

ATTRIBUTED TO ST. FRANCIS OF ASSISI, 1181–1226
FOUNDER OF THE FRANCISCAN ORDERS

Teach us to pray often; that we may pray oftener.

JEREMY TAYLOR, 1613–1667
ENGLISH WRITER AND ANGLICAN BISHOP

QUESTIONS FOR DISCUSSION AND SELF-STUDY:

1. What idols did people worship in Jesus' time? What idols do people worship today?

2. How comprehensive is the Lord's Prayer? What does it affirm?

3. Which important aspects of life does the church ritualize? How do Christian ceremonies differ from secular observances?

4. What does prayer seek? What does it affirm?

5. Can you compose a prayer that best expresses your current situation in life?

CHAPTER 7

🌿

THE BIBLE

The world into which the church was born was more literate than we imagine. Greek was a common language throughout the Roman Empire and peoples at all levels of society—slaves as well as free—could read and write. Jesus could conclude an argument with his critics by declaring, "But have you not read . . . ?" referring to the Scriptures. It was clear that they had read but had misunderstood.

Moreover, in teaching the common people Jesus assumed their acquaintance with God's teaching through the Scriptures. He would often preface his own teachings with the phrase: "It is written . . ." Among the religions of the world Christianity is unique because it was born with a Bible already in its hands. Jesus did not write Scripture, he quoted from it. More than a thousand years of God's revelation had been recorded and preserved when Jesus began to teach. The Scriptures were revered by Christian and Jew alike—a treasure to be cherished and applied to life.

The very existence of those Scriptures we now know as the Old Testament served the Jews as a bulwark against idolatry. The pagan world consistently fixed upon idols for worship, whether precious objects or representations of animals or demigods. The Jews, faithful to their invisible God, chose instead to revere a book—not as an object of worship but as the repository of revelation.

REVELATION

In Judaism strict rules governed the handling and copying of God's revelation. It was forbidden to dictate Scripture to a copier. Each new scroll had to be copied directly from another. Until the year A.D. 70, when the Temple in Jerusalem was destroyed, a master copy of the Scriptures was kept there to ensure accuracy. Each Jewish synagogue throughout the world kept its copy of the Scriptures in a cupboard positioned to face Jerusalem. Although they were never worshipped, the scrolls were considered the holiest objects in Judaism because they contained God's revelation to mankind.

To safeguard the exactness of God's word, the Scriptures were always read aloud directly from the text, never recited from memory. Throughout the ancient world to read meant to read aloud, even when one was alone reading to oneself.

Revelation was brought to life by speech. Unlike our own times, when a silent subway car can be filled with readers, the ancient world intended that what was written would be conveyed by voice. A scroll was a public treasure, not a private message, so it was shared.

Although the world of Jesus' time had become largely literate, it maintained a marked preference for the spoken word. The Greek philosopher, Plato, four centuries earlier had argued successfully that books discouraged memorization and were a poor substitute for pursuing the truth in conversation. Partly as a consequence, even the Jewish Scriptures resisted the addition of other writings for several centuries before Christ was born. Essentially, the written revelation we know as the Old Testament had ended by the time Jesus began to preach on the Scriptures. He acknowledged the revelation and came to fulfill the Scriptures, not to change them. His argument with religious authority was not with written revelation but with the hypocritical way it was being interpreted and taught—orally.

THE OLD TESTAMENT

Even when Gentiles became Christians without embracing Jewish ritual observance, they developed an almost Jewish attachment to the Scriptures that Jesus had known—the Old Testament. There they found a chronicle of God's concern surpassing any other literature. The

Bible that Jesus used consisted of twenty-four books grouped in three categories: the Law, the Prophets, and the Writings. Greek-speaking Jews of Christ's time used a version known as the Septuagint, which included seventeen more books, whole or partial. The Greek Bible distinguished between "Books of Law and History" and "Poetic and Prophetic Books."

There is no literary plan for the Old Testament except God's own plan of revelation. It is an anthology or compilation of many kinds of literature—songs, poems, historical narrative, law, ritual, prophecy, aphorisms, short stories, and cautionary tales.

Nor is the Old Testament consistently exemplary. It depicts all the sins of mankind. Its all-too-human heroes show moral frailty because God is the real protagonist. It was only natural that Jewish Christians would rely on their national sacred books. In their estimation all the hopes of the Old Testament had been fulfilled in Jesus. Although the Jewish Scriptures did not give them the articles of their creeds, it supported their belief in the Risen Lord. Responding to skeptics, Jewish Christians demonstrated the Resurrection, not from experience, but from the Book. Christ died and rose, they argued, "according to Scripture." Since it had been predicted, it must have happened!

What is more remarkable is how appealing and convincing the Jewish Scriptures in their Greek translation proved to be to the Gentiles who did not share Jewish culture. The appeal was not due to any literary charm in the text. Educated readers of the early Christian age were offended by the straightforward, unembellished style of the Septuagint, which reads more like a newspaper than literature. But this was an age that had wearied of sophistry and elaborate argument. Non-Jews were impressed by the antiquity of Hebrew Scriptures and by their simplicity and directness.

In the second century A.D., for example, the Greek philosopher Tatian discovered the Old Testament and found it to be convincing:

> When I was giving my most earnest attention to discovering the truth, I happened to meet with certain barbaric writings, too old to be compared with the opinions of the Greeks, and too divine to be compared with their errors, and I was led to put faith in these by the unpretending cast of the language, the inartificial character of the writers, the foreknowledge displayed of future events, the excellent quality of the precepts, and the declaration of the government of the Universe as centered in one Being.

Ironically, the argument from Jewish prophecy persuaded Gentiles (the non-Jewish peoples of the known world), not the Jewish nation. But the Gentiles were also moved by the high moral purpose that suffused the Old Testament—something Jews took for granted—quite refreshing to a pagan world.

The world into which Christianity was born was at once sophisticated and decadent, comfortable and cruel. Gentile Christians regarded the Jewish Scriptures as appealing to the best in mankind while condemning anything short of God's expectations of his creatures. The Scriptures were an antidote for such a moribund age.

THE NEW TESTAMENT

The early Christian community saw no need to augment the Jewish Bible it had inherited with writings of its own. The new revelation that constituted them as Christians was not written but was embodied in a person, Jesus. Eyewitnesses to the Lord, who had heard his teaching, were available to spread the Good News and they did it by preaching and traveling. A person, not a book, had formed the church.

The earliest Christians never intended that there be a written New Testament. They were fully confident that the prophecies contained in the Old Testament had been fulfilled in their own lifetimes and that Christ would return soon to inaugurate the Kingdom—probably in their lifetimes. It was imperative, therefore, to devote the short time remaining to announcing the Good News to the present generation. Living as they did "in the last days," they could not be certain that there would be another generation to leave anything to.

It was only after the eyewitnesses to Jesus' Resurrection had died, and the times lengthened, that the church realized a need to preserve the Good News in writing. Even then, word-of-mouth teaching was preferred. But, as Christianity spread, it was interpreted variously, sometimes distorted from its clear meaning. Therefore, it was imperative to defend the authentic message by referring to Apostolic witness which was now available only in writing.

The church, clearly, was not the product of Scripture but its source. Jesus wrote nothing. Rather, he founded a church to teach and save. None of the books that made their way into the New Testament was intended by its author for anything more than a specific, local, and contemporary purpose. The authors were not writing for the ages. The New Testament we know is a second-century compilation of writings, all or most of which date from Jesus' own century.

COMPILING THE
NEW TESTAMENT

It is clear from references in St. Paul's letters that written collections of Jesus' sayings had been circulating in Apostolic times. Before they were lost to history, they were used by the authors of the four gospels and by Paul himself. The Gospels—four similar accounts of Jesus' life and ministry—made their way into the New Testament. So too did the letters Paul wrote to the churches he had founded as a means of sustaining their faith when he was no longer present. Other Apostolic letters—by Peter, John, James, and Jude, as well as by the author of Hebrews, mistakenly attributed to Paul, also were judged to be reliable by the church.

An account of the earliest history of the church, the Acts of the apostles, extended the Gospel story beyond the Ascension of Jesus and dealt largely with the travels of St. Paul. Finally, apocalyptic prophecy found its way into the New Testament in the dreamlike, sometimes nightmarish, Book of Revelation or Apocalypse.

For a book unintended by its authors, the New Testament is remarkably complete and satisfying. Although the church maintained a parallel tradition of oral teaching, it has consistently recognized that the Scriptures—Old and New Testaments, taken together—contain everything a Christian needs to know to obtain salvation. As time passed following the death of the apostles, however, succeeding generations of Christian leaders found they could not equal the powerful inspiration of the New Testament authors. The great Bishop Ignatius of Antioch, for example, claimed "to speak with God's own voice," but added that he was no match for the chosen witnesses to the Resurrection: "I do not enjoin you as Peter and Paul did," he wrote; "they were Apostles . . ."

In these circumstances, the church came increasingly to treasure the Gospels and other apostolic writings it had

inherited. Indeed it needed them to defend the authentic
faith against countless revisions and heresies. The Gospels
that we know probably owe their survival to their adoption by one or another of the great church communities:
Mark's in Rome, Matthew's in Antioch, John's in Ephesus.

THE BIBLE AS WE KNOW IT

Ironically, it was a heretic's rejection of the Old Testament
that forced the church to define the New Testament. The
revisionist philosopher Marcion insisted that Old Testament revelation was unworthy of Christians, so he substituted certain books from the apostolic age on his own
authority as inspired Scripture. Not to be outdone in
fervor by a heretic, the church not only compiled a more
complete New Testament but reaffirmed the status of the
Old Testament as well.

It was not until the fourth century that the entire church
agreed on the exact contents of Christian Scripture. St.
Athanasius, having successfully composed a creed acceptable to the Council of Nicea forty-two years earlier, used
his personal authority in A.D. 367 to publish a list of
inspired books from the apostolic age. In 382 Pope Damasus called a synod in Rome which accepted St. Jerome's
plea that the New Testament as outlined by Athanasius be
confirmed. Jerome himself would provide a Latin translation of both Testaments, the Vulgate, which would serve

as the Bible of church and people for over a thousand years.

Clearly the church is not only the custodian of Scripture but also its source. Already enriched by revelation for centuries before it compiled the New Testament, the church serves as the most trustworthy interpreter of the Good News. The work of interpreting Scripture continues to our day, attempting to bring Christ's message to bear on the problems of succeeding generations. It is safe to say that, because of competent biblical scholarship, we know more about Jesus and his teaching today than did any Christians of an earlier time, with the exception of those few who literally walked with him.

It is to be expected that ancient writings not read like a book written in our time. But the Bible is amazingly straightforward and accessible; it neither hides nor holds back. It does not mystify, but explains. By definition, Scripture is revelation. Its purpose is to reveal God's love and concern and to ensure mankind's certain hope in its Savior, Jesus. The Bible is addressed to every person in every age; it is a permanent invitation to receive the promise of the Kingdom of God and to possess eternal life.

READING THE BIBLE

It is customary in American hotels, grand and humble alike, for Bibles to be provided in every room. They are placed there not by management but by a group of Christian businessmen and women, the Gideons, who know firsthand the loneliness of the traveler far from home. The Gideons have no denominational axe to grind, only a conviction that this book is literally a life preserver. At the end of a day in a strange place with no one to talk to a traveler is prone to long thoughts, and they are not always life-sustaining.

The Gideons recognize that a Bible in an impersonal hotel room can be a very personal thing. In endpapers to their edition they attempt to make the Bible speak to the needs of the man or woman who picks it up. "Are you discouraged?" "Have you suffered loss?" "Are you feeling alone?" "Are you confused?" they ask, then refer the traveler to a Bible verse or story that responds to that emotion. They intend the Bible to be read in brief passages for consolation and inspiration, but the endpapers also summarize the major revelations contained in the Bible—the stories of creation, the fall from grace, and redemption in Christ. The Gideons know the traveler doesn't have a lot of time on his hands, so they provide a simple map.

A path is needed through the Bible because it is both easy and hard to read. Easy because its language is so straightforward; difficult because the book is such a jumble of seemingly unrelated bits of literature—poetry and song, letters, sermons, narratives, histories, allegories, and genealogies. The Bible is like an attic—full of precious old things no one wants to throw away but doesn't need readily at hand. There are treasures to be found in the biblical attic and some things that can gather dust. How do you find what you need?

RULE 1. Don't start at the beginning as you would any other book, working your way through to the end. The Bible has a basic plot but you will have trouble discerning it if you just plunge in. You will find yourself diverted here and there down side roads as you proceed from book to book and may have trouble finding your way back to the main highway.

RULE 2. Don't start at the end to see how the story comes out. The last book of the Bible, Revelation, is the hardest of all to understand and it may also scare the wits out of you. Remember the Four Horsemen of the Apocalypse? They are part of the cast of Revelation and may disincline you to delve further.

RULE 3. Don't study the Bible as though it held impenetrable secrets or is infinitely subtle. There is plenty in the Bible that is unclear, but many things may have been unclear to the authors as well. Besides, the Bible doesn't try to answer all questions that interest you. The Bible is right for the ages, but each book was written for specific purposes in the past and deals immediately with that time and audience, not ours. Don't instantly demand of a passage: "What is God telling me here?" Determine first what he was telling the people at the time, then see how your situation may be similar.

RULE 4. Don't expect science or literalism or perfect consistency. The Bible contains revelation, not laboratory research. We know more about the physical world than the Bible's authors did, but that does not make us right and them wrong. Look for the moral. It is good for all time, for the wise and simple alike. Complex truths are, of themselves, no better than simple truths. Indeed simple truths tend to humble us and clear our minds and will.

RULE 5. Don't be put off by the chapter and verse numbers. These road signs were imposed on the ancient text in modern times to help people locate passages. That is their only function.

RULE 6. Don't expect to be inspired by the characters in the Bible. I know that Sunday school tends to make heroes of key characters, but even the protagonists lapse into jealousy, cruelty, greed, cowardice, and worse. Think of Abraham who passed off his wife as his sister and Peter who denied that he even knew Jesus. One of the reasons the Bible is so persuasive is that its cast of characters is so true to life, which is to say full of contradiction. But these flawed characters become heroic when, presented with hard decisions, they choose to obey God's command.

RULE 7. Do not be put off by the miraculous. See wonders as signs of God's interest and intervention. You may prefer natural explanations of the Flood, the parting of the Red Sea, and Jesus' healing the sick. What is important is to see God's hand in it. The miraculous is a sign that God cares, not that God is a Mister Fix-It, stepping in to patch up every problem. Our problems are our responsibility.

RULE 8. If you think of the Bible as a vast supermarket, you are not far wrong. But you can shop for the wrong things in it and come up with a bad diet. The devil can quote Scripture to his benefit. Generations of Jews and Christians have cited portions of the Bible as justification for their outrageous behavior. Deny the temptation to cite the Bible to support your own prejudices and rationalizations, thereby enrolling God in your righteousness. Instead, seek God's wisdom and God's will.

RULE 9. Reading and quoting the Bible is no substitute for acting on what God reveals there. The two great commandments are to love God and to love one's neighbor. All the rest is footnote.

RULE 10. Read with others who will protect you from eccentricity. Remember that the church created the Bible and it is in the church that we gain perspective on God's revelation, which speaks to us corporately, not individually.

Appendix A contains an extensive list of readings in the Bible to help you begin to acquaint yourself with its riches. The list also includes keys to discover passages in Scripture that may be familiar to you but the locations of which are not. Appendix B contains an extensive list of both the teachings of the Bible and the applications of those teachings to life. Peruse the two appendixes to see how they may be of help to you as you begin to make the Bible a book of your own.

QUESTIONS FOR DISCUSSION AND SELF-STUDY:

1. In general, what does God reveal in the Bible?

2. How does the Old Testament foreshadow the New?

3. How does the New Covenant differ from the Old?

4. Why did the New Testament text take so long to be agreed upon?

5. In which passages of the Bible does God seem to speak most clearly to you?

CHAPTER 8

THE FIRST MILLENNIUM OF FAITH

The Christian religion would likely have been little more than the pious recollection of a good man, Jesus, were it not for two events—the Resurrection and the coming of the Holy Spirit at Pentecost. "If Christ is not risen, our faith is in vain," insisted St. Paul. And if Jesus had not left his followers with his Spirit to sustain them, it is scarcely imaginable that this band of very ordinary men could have carried their faith in him to the ends of the empire, suffering persecution and death. Within less than three centuries after Jesus' death, Christianity would become the living faith of the very empire that had branded him a criminal and crucified him.

The Resurrection is the cornerstone of the Christian faith. Christ conquered death, the consequence of sin, and made good his promise that all who believe in him might live. The actual event is treated in matter-of-fact fashion in the Gospels. Early on the Sunday morning following his death, several women, including Mary, sister of Lazarus, found Jesus' tomb empty. Jesus appeared to them alive but somehow changed. Subsequently, he appeared to Peter, to the apostles, to James, and to five hundred followers at once. Last of all, Paul, who had not known Jesus in life, was confronted by the risen Christ as he was on his way to Damascus.

The sequence and sites vary in gospel accounts, but one thing is clear: Christ's followers were convinced he was not only alive but had vindicated his teaching and conquered death. The risen Christ was not an apparition. He was not ghost-like or mysterious, but fully and tangibly alive. The Apostle Thomas insisted on touching Jesus' death wound to prove he was alive. Scattered and disillusioned at his death, Jesus' followers were reunited in their experience of the risen Lord.

THE INFANT CHURCH

The beginnings of the infant church, however, would await another event that occurred fifty days after the Passover during which Jesus had been crucified. The risen Jesus had left his friends and ascended to be with the Father only a few days before. But he left with the promise that he would not leave them orphans. Commanding them to wait together in Jerusalem, he said, "You must wait for the promise made by my Father . . . you will be baptized by the Holy Spirit, and within the next few days." Gathered together in a room like the one used for the Last Supper, Jesus' followers were seized by a spirit of exaltation, as if tongues of fire had descended upon them, and received such a surge in courage and expression that they immediately began preaching the risen Christ.

According to the Acts of the Apostles, Peter was the first to speak. He called for belief in the Lord Jesus—crucified, risen, and exalted to the right hand of God. The seal of belief was Baptism by water, accompanied by an intense experience similar to theirs, which was called the Descent of the Spirit. Three thousand were converted to Christ that first day of the church's life.

The focus of the infant church remained at first in Israel, particularly in Jerusalem. Unaided by any clear indication from Jesus before he departed, the early Christians assumed he would return in their lifetimes to inaugurate the Kingdom of God in Israel. With intense expectation, the Jerusalem community awaited the Second Coming while sharing their possessions lest anyone go without. They observed the Jewish Law and worshipped in the Temple, sharing communal meals in their homes in the manner of Jesus' Last Supper with his apostles. Recalling Christ's legacy they made the Eucharist (or Thanksgiving) the focus of these meals, sharing Jesus himself in remembrance in bread and wine, and looking ahead to his return.

OPPOSITION

Although the earliest Christians were also devout Jews, they soon encountered the official opposition Jesus had experienced before them. Shortly after Pentecost Peter and his fellow apostle, John, were arrested and forbidden to preach. They refused to be silenced. Stephen, alleged to have predicted that Jesus would return to destroy both the Temple and the Law, was stoned to death. He became the first in a long line of Christian martyrs.

Rather than silencing the disciples, persecution caused them to retreat beyond the easy reach of the authorities in Jerusalem and carry the Gospel (or "good news") north to Antioch and south to Egypt. Philip traveled throughout Samaria, followed by Peter and John. Mark evangelized Egypt while Thomas went as far as India.

But the great expansion of the Christian faith was toward the west and was accomplished principally by a man who had stood by, approvingly, while Stephen was murdered for his faith in Jesus. This was Saul, a fanatical Pharisee and enforcer of pure Judaism against the Christian revisionists. On his way to discover whether the synagogue in Damascus had been infiltrated by the new faith, Saul was inexplicably struck from his horse and blinded while a voice called to him: "Saul, Saul, why do you persecute me?"

Saul's blindness was the reaction to a vision of the risen

Jesus; thus he would join the Twelve convincing all that
he, too, was a witness to the resurrected Lord and therefore an apostle. Saul became Paul, the single most imposing figure in Christianity after Jesus himself. His
importance cannot be overemphasized. Paul's letters (or
epistles) occupy nearly as many pages in the New Testament as all four Gospels combined.

PAUL'S EFFECTIVENESS

Paul was ideal in the role of apostle. Although he was a
Jew, he was nevertheless a native of Tarsus, a Greek city in
what is now Turkey. He could speak to Jews in Aramaic,
Jesus' own language, and he could preach elsewhere in
Greek, the common language of the eastern empire. Paul,
moreover, was a Roman citizen with rights to trial and
appeal to Rome. He was a citizen of the world. Exploring
the meaning of Jesus beyond the gospel accounts, Paul
scrutinized the significance of Jesus as Lord of history and
preached a new covenant in Christ. Paul was the first
theologian of the risen Lord. Critics charge that he "in-
vented" Christianity. In fact, what he did was to portray
the new faith as much more than a Jesus lifestyle. He
preached that Jeremiah's prophesy was fulfilled in Jesus. A
new covenant existed between God and man—not carved
in stone like the Ten Commandments given to Moses—
but written in men's hearts.

Paul argued that the strict Law of the Pharisees was impossible to keep perfectly; moreover, it lured observant Jews into the sins of pride and hypocrisy. Jesus had brought a new dispensation superseding the Law and embracing Jew and Gentile alike. Jesus, by carrying the sins of mankind to his death, had conquered sin and death and established a new testament (a new covenant) of freedom and love. Paul recognized that the Gentiles had been given a law of their own—the law of nature impressed in their consciences. But he knew that non-Jews failed to keep the law of nature just as the Jews failed to keep the Law of Moses.

Paul concluded that man, by his own power, is unable to keep God's law and thereby win his favor. A corruption of integrity persists in every man, woman, and child, stemming from the original sin of disloyalty. Salvation, therefore, can be achieved only by the unearned and undeserved mercy of God, offered in Christ, who suffered that mankind might live and "walk in newness of life." Paul disagreed with Peter and the original apostles by maintaining that the old precepts and ritual observances did not bind the Gentiles. One did not have to embrace strict Judaism to be a Christian. Peter, aided by a vision, agreed with Paul and immediately brought a Roman centurion into the faith.

CHRISTIANITY FREED FROM
JUDAISM

With the removal of ritual regulations, Christianity became a religion of universal appeal in which all mankind, slave or free, were brothers and sisters, so loved by their God that he had sent his Son to die to free them. This new opening to the Gentiles created a breach with Judaism that was never repaired, especially after the Christians chose Sunday, the day of the Resurrection, as their Sabbath.

The Roman Emperor Titus destroyed Jerusalem in A.D. 70. But Jewish synagogues continued to offer Paul and his followers a base in every city of importance in the empire. A common language and three hundred years of peace favored the rapid spread of the new faith. Christianity appealed to peoples everywhere. The empire had already weakened tribal and local loyalties. People felt themselves adrift in a world too large and too impersonal. The new religion offered them intimacy, community, and self-respect. Christianity made no distinction between rich and poor, Jew or Gentile, educated or unlettered. God was no respecter of persons. He loved the sinner as well as the saint.

Roman peace had been purchased at the price of boredom, at least in the cities of the empire. Freed from the burdens of war, the mobs turned to cruelty for excitement, reveling in staged combats to the death between man and man, and man and beast. Thoughtful men and women had already turned from a frantic pursuit of sensation to seek a deeper meaning in life. Many turned to superstition and a near-despairing belief in fate. Paul, sensitive to these maladies and aspirations, preached the freedom, hope, and love of the Christian faith with great success. In Jerusalem on an errand of mercy, Paul was accused of bringing Gentiles into the Temple. A riot ensued. Paul insisted on his right of appeal as a Roman citizen. After a long imprisonment, the apostle was executed under Nero.

PERSECUTION

Nero did not stop with Paul. The historian Tacitus wrote that the emperor arrested "a vast multitude of Christians":

> A sport was made of their execution. Some, sewn in the skins of animals, were torn apart by dogs. Others were crucified or burned; and others, as darkness drew on, were used as torches.

The Christians were alleged to have set fire to Rome. But Tacitus writes that the principal reason for their execution was their "hatred of the human race."

How could the loving Christians be accused of hating the human race? Because they professed loyalties the Roman world found antagonistic. Christians refused to worship the emperor or to kill in military service. Christians kept to their own communities, spurning the popular bread-and-circus atmosphere. Their exclusiveness and other-worldliness prompted people to view them with suspicion. It became widely rumored that in the celebration of the Eucharist Christians sacrificed human life and devoured the victims.

Paul had counseled Christians to respect Roman law and custom as far as possible in the expectation that Jesus' imminent return would alter the entire order of society. Because Jesus would soon make the changes, Paul reasoned, Christians should not bother to alter their own status, whether rich or poor, slave or free, married or unmarried.

Church organization was informal but serviceable. Functions were exercised by those with specific gifts bestowed by the Holy Spirit—preachers, healers, teachers, and administrators. Each local community was largely governed by those members possessing these gifts. But appointments were also made—deacons to minister to the poor and presbyters (or priests) to preside at the Lord's Supper. Moreover, it required a council of church leaders to decide, for the whole church, that Christians were freed from Jewish law. Paul supervised all the communities he had founded, a function similar to that of modern bishops.

ORGANIZATION

From the beginning the pattern of church life was set with priests and deacons ministering to local communities and bishops ensuring peace regionally among a number of communities and with councils of church leaders settling doctrinal disputes.

In Rome another tradition was in the making. The origins of the Roman Church are clouded, but it is certain that both Peter and Paul were present to nurture its growth. As Rome was the hub of the empire, so it became the center of the church. For fifteen centuries the bishops of Rome would be recognized as enjoying apostolic succession from Peter to whom Jesus had given the keys of the Kingdom of Heaven. Catholics still recognize the preeminence of the bishop of Rome, better known as the pope.

CHRISTIANITY BECOMES A WORLD RELIGION

The fourth century began with a convulsive effort by the Roman Empire to rid itself once and for all of the Christian church. Diocletian, a patriot general fresh from defending Rome's borders against the barbarians, became emperor. In a swift series of moves he set about reclaiming Rome's glory by restoring its pagan gods. Although at the time they comprised no more than 10 percent of the population in the West, the Christians were identified as those most likely to dissent to the pagan restoration.

Accordingly in the year 303 Diocletian ordered every church destroyed and every copy of the Scriptures burned. He stripped Christians of their citizenship and the protection of the laws. When his invitation to repent went unheeded, the emperor decreed death for every Christian. In the space of a little more than a year Diocletian's bloodbath so swelled the ranks of martyrs that there were no longer enough days in the Christian calendar to commemorate them. Then, abruptly, in the year 305 the emperor retired his office and the last great persecution ended in the West, although it would flare up over the next twenty years in the East.

Diocletian's voluntary retirement was a high-principled attempt to ensure an orderly transfer of power in the empire. Before leaving the scene he decentralized authority throughout the imperial lands to discourage usurpers and created lines of succession in East and West. An "augustus" was to reign in the East; another in the West. Each ruler would appoint a second-in-command or "caesar" who would succeed to imperial authority upon the death or retirement of the augustus. In turn, they would name their own successors while they lived.

As planned, the caesar of the West, Constantius Chloris, succeeded as augustus, but when he died his son, Constantine, refused to acknowledge the new caesar, claiming the West for himself as a birthright. Taking command of the armies of Britain and Gaul, Constantine initiated a series of wars in which six men would vie for the power of the empire, both West and East. Placing himself under the patronage of Apollo, the sun-god, Constantine prepared to move against Rome itself.

As he mobilized his troops, Constantine had a dream or vision of a cross in the sky bearing the following legend: "By this sign, conquer." Without hesitation, in a conversion as stunning as St. Paul's, the Roman proclaimed himself a Christian and marched successfully on Rome under what he called a "divine impulse," becoming master of the Western world in the year 312 and of the entire empire a dozen years later.

In the space of six years the Roman Empire was transformed from persecutor of Christians to Christian! Although Constantine tolerated all religions, he proclaimed himself "God's man," the successor to generations of martyrs, claiming victory not by death but through combat. He became the first of the Christian rulers to identify himself as the instrument of God's purpose on earth.

THE NEW ORDER

Constantine's conversion defies explanation. There was no political advantage for him to take the part of a small minority of dissenters. But convert he did. Constantine abandoned the pretension of the caesars to divinity. And when church disputes were brought to him for a decision, he asked why judgment should be expected of him since the emperor awaited the judgment of God like every other man. The new Christian emperor made the Christian Sabbath a holiday but, in a lingering nod to his former protector, Apollo, he called it, not the Lord's Day, but Sun-day. More dramatically, three centuries after the death of Jesus on the cross, Constantine ended the Roman practice of crucifixion.

United until now in opposition to arms, Christians increasingly came to regard Constantine's battles as holy wars like those of the kings of the old Testament. Bishop Eusebius of Caesarea would claim that Constantine, in reconciling the pagan kingdoms to the one true God, was fulfilling the promise of Isaiah that swords should be beaten into plowshares and nations should learn war no more. Constantine's peace-through-war was, however, only temporary. Henceforth, Christians could no longer be radical pacifists, leaving war to the pagans, but would have to seek the way of justice in man's disputes with man.

Constantine had hopes that his new faith would cement the empire. He was to be gravely disappointed, for the church took advantage of imperial toleration and privilege to revive its own parochial disputes. In North Africa a Christian majority refused to recognize those priests who had handed over the Scriptures to Diocletian rather than imperil Christian lives. These rigorists were called Donatists after their leader, Bishop Donatus. When Constantine sought to restore church property in Africa, the Donatists claimed it as their own. Constantine first referred the matter to the pope, who decided against the rigorists. When the Donatists defied the pope, Constantine summoned a council of Western bishops who met at Arles in Gaul in 314. The council supported the pope's decision but to no avail. Unyielding, the Donatists appealed to Constantine himself, who confirmed both pope and council but was unable to subdue the dissident Christians.

CHURCH AUTHORITY

The drama, however, established an important principle. The Christian ruler, henceforth, was committed to deferring to pope and council in strictly religious matters. A more serious dispute broke out in the East, this time striking not at discipline, but at the heart of the Christian faith. In Egypt the priest Arius sought to make Jesus more congenial by claiming that Christ was a creature—a model for man, but himself no more than a man. Arius's antagonist in Alexandria, the deacon Athanasius, argued that man's salvation required the identity of Jesus the Son with God the Father. He insisted that if Jesus were not one with the Father then there was no way for mere creatures like ourselves to be united with God. Arius, in attempting to make Christ more human, risked making Jesus another pagan demigod, a hero of flesh and blood alone.

It is difficult to image the vehemence of religious

disputes in the everyday lives of Christians of the time. But evidence abounds. Arius roused even the stevedores on the Alexandria docks with his preaching of the "human" Christ. Neither the Scriptures nor the traditional teaching of the church could convincingly resolve the dispute. Both the Bible and the early theologians could be quoted to support either position. So again reference was made to a council of bishops which met at Nicea in present-day Turkey in the year 325. Unlike earlier gatherings it included great numbers of church leaders from the East as well as the West and has since been known as the first of the ecumenical (or universal) councils.

The Council of Nicea sided with the Athanasians in composing a creed still voiced by Christians as their profession of faith. Constantine complied by banishing Arius.

AN INTERNATIONAL INSTITUTION

Heretofore a community of faith linking local congregations, the Christian church now had become a vast public institution inclined to look to Roman law and imperial administration for models of government. Later, generations of Catholic Christians would wonder at the weighty and intricate bodies of church law, and the inclination of popes and bishops to rule by decree rather than by precedent and the consent of the faithful. But the church had no other civilized models of administration to follow except that of Rome. In subsequent centuries, the church would oppose the arbitrary rule of kings; yet only when political democracy and common law gained favor in our own time would the church temper its Roman style of rule in favor of local autonomy, representative government, and the rule of precedent in law. The Reformation that began in the sixteenth century would seek to return to first-century simplicity but with rare success. Christianity had become an organized colossus.

For many Christians the recognition of the church by the empire was a mixed blessing. Respectability ended martyrdom and invited complacency. Accordingly, zealots fled the cities to form new, economically self-sufficient communities devoted to simplicity, prayer, and self-sacrifice. Whereas the early Christian communities consisted of natural families, these new monastic communities were composed of celibate adults dedicated to a shared life devoted to God's glory and prayer for all God's people. The monks in their rude monasteries would preserve Christian scholarship as well as classical culture through the long centuries of barbarism—the Dark Ages.

MONKS AND MISSIONARIES

Far from being escapists, Christian monks became the great missionaries to the barbarian tribes of the north and east. Their physical needs were simple and they traveled unencumbered by families. Journeying to strange lands in twos and threes, the monks would settle to till the soil, building new monasteries with their hands in the midst of the barbarians.

Less than a century after Constantine embraced Christianity for the empire, Rome fell to the barbarians. In 410 an army of Visigoths under Alaric devastated the Eternal City. The capital of the empire had already been moved to Constantinople (modern Istanbul). This second Rome would hold out for another thousand years. But a dream had been shattered when the city of the caesars expired. It was as if civilization itself had died. The barbarian invasions of Europe continued for six hundred years. During these long centuries the entire Western world lived in a state of siege from a series of primitive peoples who moved in such numbers that they created whole nations as they settled.

They came not because they were attracted to the wealth and sophistication of the empire, but because they were themselves displaced by even stronger tribes in the East. The barbarians were no more savage than the cruel Romans nor was the nomadic life natural to them; rather, they were rustics looking for a place to settle and farm. The "invasions" actually represented the breakdown of orderly migration that had been controlled by Rome for centuries.

CHRISTIAN CULTURE

If indeed a dream had ended with Rome's fall, civilization remained. To be sure, a sophisticated culture was buried, not to be disinterred until the Renaissance. Art, literature, and architecture were immediate victims. But the decline of the West can be overexaggerated. Imperial Rome had been in decline for centuries. Art and literature had become mannered. Philosophy was effete and despairing. Architecture was obsessed by ornamentation. Tyrants ruled in place of law. Sensitivity had degenerated into sensuality. The city that fell to the barbarians was the Rome of bread and circuses.

When Rome, the center not only of empire but of Christian orthodoxy, fell, a Christian explanation was required. It came from St. Augustine, bishop of Hippo in North Africa, and the most influential Christian thinker since St. Paul himself. Augustine blamed Rome's destruction on its cruelty and corruption, quoting the remark of a Briton, "The Romans make a desert and call it peace." Every empire deserves destruction because it is dominated by lust for power. Nations are no better rising than falling and God inevitably brings them down in his own good time.

Although he was witness to a great calamity, Augustine was not tempted to see it with the eyes of the earliest Christians. It was not the end of the world. Instead,

Augustine took the long view that, until Christ returned in the indefinite future, it fell upon the church itself to ensure justice and to approximate the kingdom of God on earth. Rome was overrun, but the church prevailed. Monasteries became safe communities of prayer, learning, and welfare, from which monks ventured to convert the barbarians. Where the imperial authority failed, the church succeeded in caring for the needs of the people and establishing civil order. Pope Gregory the Great (590–604) chartered ships to bring food from Sicily and Sardinia and set about sheltering the refugees and rebuilding the city. He ransomed hostages and negotiated treaties with the invaders.

Gregory was successful in this work of rehabilitation because the church had resources: farms, forests, property, and money. Jesus had preached that it is easier for a camel to pass through the eye of a needle than for a rich man to enter the Kingdom of God. As a consequence, there was a great divesting of personal wealth by Christians, notably to the church at Rome. Instead of giving directly to the poor or caring personally for the sick, wealthy Christians gave to the church, which became a great philanthropic organization.

ISLAM AND THE DARK AGES

With the West at its weakest, a new threat came from the East, doubly potent because it combined the power of arms and religion. In seventh-century Arabia a camel driver, Mohammed, combined elements of Judaism and Christianity into a simplified faith, Islam, which promised sensuous salvation to the disciplined and called for Holy War to unite the Arab world. Islam swept through the East to the gates of Constantinople, through North Africa, Spain, and into France, producing a culture of such sophistication that it would not only preserve the classics but improve on them.

With Islam at its borders Europe was mired in barbarian struggles. These were the Dark Ages covering roughly the three centuries from 800 to 1100. The entire population of Europe was obsessed with sheer survival. Scandinavian Vikings terrorized Britain and the continent by land and sea while the Magyars spread from the East. Christian kings attempted to protect their tenant farmers (with no notable success) in return for fealty. This was the beginning of the feudal system of mutual obligations of lord and vassal.

The effectiveness of the church in ensuring peace and justice was unavoidably uneven. Unlike the hereditary lines of kings, popes were subject to election and therefore to the whims of politics. Fortunately, Christianity retained vitality through the Dark Ages by way of the monasteries. The new monasteries became civilizing influences throughout Europe. Unlike their insular predecessors, the new monks were outward-looking, intent on making Christian ideals transform secular society.

With Europe only just emerging from the Dark Ages, Pope Urban II, a former monk, reached for a common cause to unite Christendom. The Eastern emperor had called for help in subduing the Islamic Turks. Using the request as pretext the pope called for a holy war or Crusade to protect the Christian East and to rescue the Holy Land from the Moslems. Four years later a mostly French army entered the city of Jerusalem in a sea of infidel blood, singing that Christ had conquered.

QUESTIONS FOR DISCUSSION AND SELF-STUDY:

1. What was it about Christianity that threatened the civilized Roman world?

2. Why did Christianity enjoy more success with Gentiles than with Jews?

3. Was an institutional church necessary to sustain the Christian faith?

4. How could a Christianized Europe be more barbaric than the Roman Empire it succeeded?

5. What was accomplished by monks and monasteries?

CHAPTER 9

THE SECOND MILLENNIUM OF FAITH

THE HIGH MIDDLE AGES

Fully eleven centuries after the birth of Jesus, it began to appear that a truly Christian society was possible. The Vikings, last of the barbarian invaders, had embraced the faith of Christ. For the first time in six hundred years Europe felt sufficiently secure for nobles to leave their lands and carry sword and cross to the East. Because of the Crusade Jerusalem for the first time became the center of a Christian nation. The cross of victory would be raised over the Holy City for two centuries.

At last the Dark Ages were at an end. A new light penetrated every aspect of life—economic, artistic, architectural, political, and intellectual, as well as religious. The world was in flower. Europe, since Rome's destruction a continent of villages, now—with peace—fostered the growth of cities. Trading replaced raiding and a substantial merchant class developed. Cities became sites for universities, some eighty of them founded in the twelfth and thirteenth centuries alone. Canon law was codified by Gratian ensuring consistent administration of the Christian church in all nations. The sophisticated Roman civil law of Justinian was rediscovered and applied throughout Europe, supplanting Germanic tribal law.

INTELLIGENCE AND CHIVALRY

Theology and philosophy enjoyed a revival that underscored a renewed confidence in the power of the human mind such as had not existed since the time of Plato and Aristotle centuries before Christ. While Scholasticism acknowledged that revelation was beyond reason, this new method analyzed truth and exposed superstition with a rigor similar to the scientific method of modern times. For over a thousand years Christianity had been winning mankind's hearts and souls. Now, in the high Middle Ages, it appealed to minds and even began to make a difference in behavior.

The ideal of chivalry caught the imagination of the Christian nobility. While it did not temper their ferocity, it made them aware of their duty to defend the weak and induced them to concentrate their violence on jousting tourneys rather than whimsical wars. Chivalry was not Christian in origin, nor was the blossoming interest in romantic love; yet, because they represented refinements in behavior after centuries of barbarism, they encouraged the spread of Christian idealism.

The medieval resurgence of romantic love can be traced to Islamic influences. Typically it took the form of a passionate but unconsummated ardor of a knight for a married woman. At first marriage was despised by the new spirit of romance because it was so often contracted solely to ensure the inheritance of property. Nevertheless, in time the bond between husband and wife became appreciated throughout Christendom as not just an economic contract, but a sacrament of love, symbolic of Christ's love for his church.

MONKS AND CRUSADERS

As love flowered in secular life, so did the life of Christian denial in monastic life. The medieval monasteries originally founded to make the world more Christian had themselves become worldly and needed reform. St. Bernard of Clairvaux in the twelfth century called for a return to the literal observance of the Rule of St. Benedict, restoring the monks to prayer and manual labor and monasteries to economic self-sufficiency. His Cistercian monks became such scientific farmers and herders that they enriched the agricultural economy of Europe.

Bernard himself was the most arresting religious figure

of the century. Possessed of a towering intellect and profound spirituality, he was at the same time a forceful statesman. When a papal election was disputed, Bernard personally convinced every European monarch to support the better candidate, Innocent II. Unable to pacify the warrior nobles of Europe, Bernard began to turn their aggression to better use. Bernard's own monastic rule was partly adopted by the crusaders known as the Knights of the Temple. But as new Crusades were mounted, they began to attract the dregs of European society—mercenary adventurers. The second and third Crusades were failures. The fourth Crusade ended with the Christian army invading and looting Christian Constantinople itself, the defense of which had been the original justification for the Holy Wars. The last Christian stronghold in the Holy Land fell to the Turks in 1291, almost two centuries after the triumphal entry of the Christian knights into Jerusalem.

MAN'S SINS, GOD'S GLORY

The spiritual sophistication of the twelfth century was dramatized by the rise of Gothic architecture, a dizzying denial of gravity itself, with spires and arches lifting the spirit and penetrating the heavens. The new Gothic style was not wholly optimistic, however. Rather, it represented the straining of man's spirit against the weight of his sins.

The high Middle Ages, for all its optimism, was notable for its sense of sin. Gone was the naive brutality of the Dark Ages. Consequently, with life safer and less austere, Christians learned to take some blame upon themselves for the world's evil. The devil in all his demonic disguises was everywhere portrayed. Man's sins and God's glory were dramatized within the cathedrals in stained glass, statuary, and the stations of the cross.

For the illiterate the cathedrals were both storybooks and sermons. They were also meeting houses, theaters, and markets. Only the sanctuary of each church was off-limits to the commerce of everyday life. The cathedrals were treasured by their communities and literally built by the people. To construct the magnificent Chartres in France the townspeople—nobles to commoners, adults to children—harnessed themselves to carts to haul the cathedral's building blocks.

The administration of justice was still severe but more evenhanded as secular and Christian law came to touch aspects of life heretofore either tolerated or punished by death. Often conflicting with civil authority, the church defended the right of women to inherit property and prohibited interest-bearing loans, judging them contrary to Christian charity.

THE IMITATION OF CHRIST

Feeling themselves far from the time of Christ, medieval Christians sought to restore the simplicity of primitive Christianity. St. Francis of Assisi believed literally in the imitation of Christ and God's watchful providence. He and his followers embraced poverty, begging for the barest necessities and living as wretchedly as the poorest of God's creatures. Prohibited from teaching in churches and schools because of their lack of formal training, Franciscan friars became itinerant preachers of love and hope, of gentleness and concern, walking as Jesus and the apostles had to find anyone who would listen to the Good News. The Spaniard, St. Dominic, complemented the work of Francis. Just as poor and mobile, his followers became great teachers, feeding Christian minds as Francis had fed their hearts.

As the behavior of Christians improved there were those who thought the pace too slow and attempted their own brand of perfection. The Waldensians embraced Franciscan poverty but scorned the clergy and eventually became outlaws, hewing to the literal words of the Bible, forsaking oaths, the protection of their families, and the artifacts of devotion (which they deemed idols). The Albigensians revived the old Manichaean heresy which construed all creation as evil. In their attempts to create a pure Christianity the new heretics rejected Christ's human nature, the sacraments, all images of devotion, and the authority of the visible church. Forced eventually to admit they could not escape their bodies, the Albigensians concluded absurdly that, since sin was inevitable, it did not matter. Thus their search for perfection led to riotous irresponsibility.

To rid the Christian people of these fanatical heretics, Pope Gregory IX in 1233 assembled a corps of learned friars to judge false teachers. Thus began the Inquisition, conceived innocently to ensure consistent preaching, but easily twisted by Europe's rulers to justify political purges.

LOGIC, LITERATURE, AND DECLINE

The pinnacle of Christian culture was reached in the thirteenth century, notably by a Dominican philosopher and theologian, Thomas Aquinas, and an Italian poet, Dante Alighieri. The one by logic, the other by literature, constructed schemes of the universe that ranged from heaven to hell, governed by God's providence.

The fourteenth century undid the civilizing work of the previous two centuries. The church, heretofore master of the high Middle Ages, now became a victim of power politics and a new spirit of barbarism. As the ruling houses of Europe solidified their power, Christianity was required to focus attention on defending church property and rights in each nation. Spiritual influence was no longer sufficient against power politics. The bishop of Rome in self-defense aped the monarchies and became a monarch of a state that levied taxes and hired mercenary armies.

The fourteenth century, moreover, was no time to live; it was a time to die. Fully one-third of Europe's population expired horribly from a plague carried by rats and known as the Black Death. Europe's fine new cities became breeding grounds for the rats; at times not enough people in a neighborhood were left alive even to bury the huge numbers of dead neighbors. The century was also plagued by war—the Hundred Years' War, fought largely by mercenary soldiers who offered their services to the highest bidder and had no respect for noncombatants. Adversity brought out the worst in the Christian population. In the plague, parents deserted their own children. In the war, nobles deserted their vassals. There was no public spirit, no public service, and no protection from rats and soldiers. Whole villages died. Europe became a wasteland of ghost towns, pillaged by bands of marauders.

To pay for their wars England and France taxed the church and expropriated its property within their borders. Pope Boniface VIII lashed out declaring that the power of kings comes not directly from God but through the church. Threatened with excommunication, Philip the Fair of France sent henchmen to capture the pope, who died of their mistreatment. Philip effectively became master of the church, moving it from Rome to Avignon in

France for the years 1305 to 1378. Because the Avignon popes were virtual prisoners, they were forced to find ways to compensate for the loss of income from the abandoned church lands around Rome.

BAD CHOICES, THREE POPES

An unhappy choice was the wide-scale dispensation of indulgences. Purporting to control the keys of the kingdom granted to Peter, the church remitted some of the purifying punishment for past sins that penitent Christians expected to undergo after death before being admitted to heaven. Strictly speaking indulgences were not sold by the church; and some good works were expected before they were granted. In practice, however, the "good works" consisted of a few prayers, and monetary offerings were clearly expected. Ironically, as the captive papacy declined in influence it grew in wealth.

In 1377 Pope Gregory XI asserted church independence from France and returned to Rome. His cardinals, however, remained in France and elected a substitute who took the name Clement VII. At first Europe's rulers took advantage of two competing popes to consolidate further their hold on clergy and property. But even in political decline, the church was too pervasive to be toyed with internationally. Rival bishops arose in each nation taking the part of Gregory or the pretender, thus creating civil confusion.

Treaties and marriages between royal families were forestalled because they happened to support the Roman pope or the French antipope. Finally, in 1409 cardinals from Rome and Avignon assembled at Pisa, deposed both papal contenders, and elected a substitute. But rather than resolve the problem this attempt at a solution only produced a third pretender. The matter was finally resolved in 1414 when a church council organized by nations at Constance elected Martin V while deposing two pretenders and accepting the resignation of the third.

DECLINE AND REFORMATION

The church had turned to power politics in self-defense. Having failed miserably it had its authority restored, ironically, by its enemies who needed to use it. But the church's moral influence had been sapped through scandal. When society was ripe again for religious reform, the Protestants would look to the state, not the church, to support them.

Ever since Europe emerged from the Dark Ages in the twelfth century there had been a chronic cry for reform within the church. Popes, councils, and kings lamented the ignorance and venality of the clergy, but to no avail. Unhappily, the institutional church was so interwoven with the fabric of secular life that it could scarcely be distinguished from the society it served. The church had lifted Europe out of centuries of barbarism only to become assimilated into the world it tried to reform.

During those bleak centuries when kings had neglected to protect and care for their subjects, the church had assumed the task. In turn, generations of grateful Christians willed their wealth to the church to be distributed to the poor and to care for the sick. Since much of this wealth was in land, the church of the Middle Ages had unwittingly become a political force, possessing by the year 1500 at least one-fifth and perhaps as much as one-third of the real estate of Europe.

A dedicated, spiritual clergy might have continued to employ the church's power for good by selling the land and distributing the proceeds to allay poverty and suffering. But wealth and power lured a different sort of person to the religious life. Since all property in a medieval family passed directly to the first-born son, subsequent male children were forced to shift for themselves to earn a living. The second son traditionally sought his fortune by becoming a soldier; the third by becoming a priest. There was no sense of "calling" to a life of religious service, excepting the poor monks and mendicants. For the prospective priest, it was simply another way to make a living and literally a third-rate way at that. Expectations were low all around; so was performance.

CELIBACY AND CONCUBINAGE

Following the monastic ideal, the church expected its clergy to refrain from marriage. An unmarried priest, freed from family responsibilities, could devote himself to a life of prayer and care for his parish. An unmarried priesthood also made economic good sense. A single priest was only a modest burden on his flock for his necessities. Furthermore, if it was guaranteed that he would have no children, the priest could not pass church property to his offspring by way of inheritance. This was the theory. In practice many priests lived in open concubinage, especially scandalous because such liaisons were overtly sensual at a time when marriage was contracted for responsible business reasons. A visitation of the English diocese of Hereford by its bishop in 1397 revealed fifty-two clergy out of 281 parishes had concubines. Another in Lausanne on the Continent in 1416 recorded eighty priests living in flagrant concubinage in a diocese of 273 parishes.

The new monastic communities and the mendicant friars had introduced a reforming spirit to the church. Inevitably, however, once the generation of their founders had died out, the new orders themselves attracted wealth and the wrong kind of monk and friar. Hope was flickering; decline and decadence seemed inevitable. There were reformers but no comprehensive and lasting reform. The church was overripe and decaying. Competing popes had morally discredited the papacy. Pope Alexander VI would father four children, two of them evil incarnate—Cesare and Lucretia Borgia.

For a time it appeared that church councils were the remedy. The Council of Constance had deposed popes and pretenders, and reestablished the line of conciliar authority. But the Council of Basel destroyed that hope. Summoned in 1431 to deal with the uproar throughout Bohemia after the burning of the reformer Jan Huss, the council chose a policy of appeasement and containment. The German emperor was unable to defeat the Hussite armies. Basel made a theological accommodation based on this military fact: it allowed the Hussite heresy to be tolerated in those districts where it prevailed. This precedent cracked the unity of Christian teaching and would weigh in the political calculations of the Protestant reformers already on the horizon.

THE SURRENDER OF CONSTANTINOPLE

While the council was still in session a great opportunity and challenge presented itself. Constantinople was besieged by the Moslem Turks and pleaded to pope and council for aid. Their reply was to demand compliance of Orthodox churches with the Western Creed before aid would be given. When theological blackmail failed to bring around the Eastern Church to the Western Creed, military assistance was withheld and Constantinople, the city of Constantine and the last vestige of the Eastern Roman Empire, surrendered to Islam in 1453.

The church, having sought to conquer the world for Christ, had become worldly. It was, to be sure, no worse than the world it had hoped to convert, but only insufficiently better. Spirituality was at low ebb. The sense of sin that had pervaded the faithful during the high Middle Ages persisted ever more acutely in the centuries of decline. But now, rather than impelling sinners to goodness, it mired them in despair. At the dawn of the Reformation Europe had endured a century of plague and total war, a drama of depravity and despair. Faith looked in vain for charity; now hope itself was dying. Reform, when it came, would disregard the international Catholic Church, creating instead local and national religious communities gathered in the name of Christ, each claiming the simplicity and inspiration of the first Christians.

These new Protestant communities would shed not only the political pretensions of the Catholic Church but also its internationalism and universality. Confining themselves to Christian communities on a scale similar to those of the first century, the Protestants would endear themselves to Europe's rulers who at last could expropriate church property and consolidate their own authority in their own lands without the interference of organized faith. The Protestant Reformation gathered adherents and defenders because it narrowed the definition and role of the church of Christ. The Catholic Church conceived its role as the kingdom of God on earth, embracing and directing every aspect of life, however mundane; the Reformers would settle for a church that was a community of worship and mutual assistance.

LUTHER

The reform wrought by the German friar Martin Luther illustrates how resistant the Catholic Church was to reform and how ripe Europe was for an alternative to Rome. Ironically, Luther's original intention was only to reform himself. Overwhelmed by the majesty and wrath of God, young Martin reviled himself as "dust and ashes and full of sin." At the age of twenty-one he sought relief from his inner torment through a life of service to God and by severe self-denial and confessions lasting as long as six hours at a stretch. Eventually he concluded that nothing he could do could satisfy God.

To distract Luther's attention from his sins, his confessor assigned him to teach theology at the University of Wittenberg and to preach in the parish church. But it was only at the edge of despair that Luther came to terms with his own unworthiness—when he threw himself upon Jesus' mercy, accepting God's goodness through faith alone.

A master of rustic metaphor, Luther characterized sinful

man as dung covered by God's grace as by a blanket of snow. If man could not change, then what was critical was the sinner's willingness to trust and accept the Savior. Equally critical was man's knowledge of God's promises and expectations which was to be found unaltered in the Bible. This was not reform; it was a redefinition of religion and it made the church redundant. For Luther, the Rock was not the church, but a book; and the drama of salvation was individual rather than societal.

Luther sprang to prominence in 1517 when he objected publicly to the peddling of indulgences. Outrageous claims were made for indulgences by the Dominican friar Johann Tetzel. Not only would they remit the penalties for sin, but remove the sins themselves and the punishment for sins not yet committed. Worse, if possible, was Tetzel's claim made on behalf of those relatives and friends already dead: "As soon as the coin in the coffer rings, the soul from Purgatory springs."

Luther objected that if the church had such power it should free all Christians from Purgatory in one stroke. He insisted, however, that forgiveness came only from the self-sacrifice of Jesus. This, he argued, was a truth of the Bible that did not require the mediation or administration of the church. His debate used indulgences as an issue to strike at the authority of the Catholic Church. Although Luther was given a fair hearing by church leaders, he had drawn the line on doctrinal rather than moral grounds and there could be no resolution. The Catholic Church might admit to scandal but not to irrelevancy.

LUTHER PROTECTED

Luther escaped death at the stake because his protector, Frederick the Wise, was the pope's choice for election as German emperor. Germany, in the sixteenth century, was a conglomeration of some three hundred principalities, each jealous of its rights, with no overall authority to tame a preacher of Luther's spirit. While the pope tarried in preparing a condemnation of Frederick's protegé, Luther made a grass-roots appeal to the German princes to reject the church's pretensions in their territories. He then widened his breach with Rome by insisting that the church could not exclude anyone from the sacraments because all believers were priests, dealing directly with God.

Popes had long held the power to ban Europe's rulers from the sacraments and the churches in their own realms. Luther was offering kings and princes freedom from papal excommunication, a weapon intended to discredit rulers before their subjects. In addition Luther claimed that Jesus was no more revealed in the sacramental rites than he was in the Gospel. When the Spaniard Charles I became German emperor, he found he could not act on his personal authority to condemn Luther but was required to consult the German princes. By this time Luther was so popular a national figure that all parties aimed at appeasement to avert a civil war.

A NEW CHURCH AND NEW CHURCHES

By 1522 Luther was no longer the reformer of the existing church but effectively the administrator of a new Christian church. Catholic services would continue in Luther's Wittenberg for two more years, then be outlawed altogether. At Strasbourg in the 1520s the Catholic Mass was celebrated at the altar but Lutheranism was preached from the pulpit. Before the decade was out four more German princes embraced Lutheranism and moved to eject the Catholic Church from their territories. Pope and emperor were busy elsewhere and unable to move politically or militarily against the German reformers.

In 1529 the principal German princes called for a church council to include the Lutherans, proposing that Lutherans tolerate Catholics within their own territories while excluding Lutherans altogether from Catholic areas. The Lutheran princes protested and thereby gave the reform movement its name: Protestant. Loosed from Catholic tradition, Protestants inclined to individual interpretation of the Bible. Luther believed that Christ's teachings were sufficiently clear to create consensus in any case.

Other reformers proved him wrong. In Switzerland Zwingli and Calvin had been leading reform in the churches of their respective cities, Zurich and Geneva. On various points of doctrine and practice they differed from Luther and from each other and proceeded to set their own directions. In 1531, Luther reluctantly agreed to the death penalty for yet another Protestant sect, the Anabaptists, who believed the Gospel required them to be pacifists. Pacifism did not have a chance in this turbulent clash of faiths. Religious persecutions pitted Protestant against Catholic and Protestant against Protestant. Religious toleration would come only after centuries when it became apparent that no one sect could prevail and when rulers learned to prefer civil concord to religious bickering.

In England the Reformation movement was used as pretext for Henry VIII to reject his role as vassal to the pope and assert his own authority over the Catholic Church in his realm and, not surprisingly, to expropriate its property. Doctrine and morality were not the driving motives. Power was. By midcentury what had begun as an attempt to reform the Catholic Church had ended by creating many churches and substituting kings for popes.

COUNTER-REFORMATION

At the same time as Northern Europe was locked in the agonies of the Protestant revolt, Italy was enjoying a Renaissance of art and culture unmatched since Greece and Rome at the height of their civilizations. To Luther, sinful man was a worm. But to Michelangelo and Leonardo da

Vinci even tragic man was heroic and woman in her sorrow was beautiful.

While the reformers focused on the agony of the Godman in the act of Redemption, the Roman Church celebrated the smiling Infant Jesus at the Madonna's breast. Whatever reform might be possible within the church, there was to be no reconciliation between two attitudes so opposed.

A council was called at Trent in 1545 to deal with the Protestant threat, but it was too late to reunite Christianity. Doctrinal disputes and political considerations now overshadowed the original requirement for moral reform. Moreover, Rome feared a repetition of the Council of Constance, which had deposed one pope, elected another, and thoroughly intimidated his immediate successors. Through brilliant diplomacy, however, the papacy utterly contained the council, requiring papal approval for every decree and reserving to the pope the sole right to interpret the council's decisions. After a brief appearance, Lutherans who hoped to influence the council acknowledged the pope's command of the stage and left.

Trent dragged through three sessions in as many years. Rather than make any accommodation with the reformers, the council further defined traditional Catholic teaching to accentuate real differences. It ended the worst moral abuses by administrative reform and centralization of authority in the Vatican, not by appeals to Christlike behavior by priests and bishops.

Probably Trent's most effective legacy was its determination to instill a consistency in celebrating the Eucharist. Until the council put a stop to it, the reenactment of the Last Supper and Jesus' self-sacrifice suffered the whims of local priests and was too often eccentric, superstitious, and vulgar. To dramatize the literal universality of its worship, the council insisted that the Mass be celebrated in the Latin language everywhere in the world according to minutely precise procedures which stood unchallenged until the Second Vatican Council in the 1960s.

THE JESUITS AND THE AGE OF ENLIGHTENMENT

A new religious community now emerged admirably suited to the needs of a Catholic Church on the counteroffensive. Ignatius of Loyola was a former soldier devoted to changing men's minds and hearts for God. His followers, the Jesuits, placed themselves directly at the disposal of the pope and became great teachers and missionaries. They spearheaded the Counter-Reformation, returning Poland, parts of France, Germany, and the Netherlands to traditional Catholicism, and at the same time carrying Christ to the Orient and to the New World. As the reform movement splintered, the Catholic Church pulled together.

The defeat of the Spanish Armada in 1588 and the

inconclusiveness of the Thirty Years' War in the following century dramatized the new balance between Protestant and Catholic Europe. A Cold War began which no one could win. From 1650 until nearly the end of the nineteenth century the Catholic Church was in a state of siege, concerned with devoting its substantial remaining power to ensure the purity of the traditional faith and the discipline of its clergy and faithful. In Catholic lands the Inquisition continued for a time to suppress dissent. But a new threat came not from Protestant reformers but from a new breed of thinkers who chose to look at the universe and at man himself without reference to either church or Bible, relying instead on their experience and their minds to discover the truth. Catholics and Protestants alike faced the Age of Enlightenment.

Galileo, one of the new men of science, was also a man of faith. "The authority of Sacred Scripture," he wrote, "has as its sole aim to convince men of those truths which are necessary for their salvation. But that the same God who has endowed us with reason and understanding should not wish us to use them—this is a thing I do not think I am bound to believe."

The Catholic Church judged differently. The aged scientist, shown instruments of torture used by the Inquisition, backed down from publishing his findings. For the church fearful of losing its authority, it was a shallow victory; it could not suppress science and reason. Unwittingly, the church had itself become a prisoner to the

ancient Greek writer, Aristotle, whose philosophy expressed Catholic theology well but whose science was
naive and, in many cases, utterly wrong. It would not be
until 1992 that the church admitted its error.

JANSENISM

As the Catholic Church resisted scientific optimism from
without, it was challenged by theological pessimism from
within. Although it was unrelated to Protestantism the
new pessimism shared a similar belief in the corruption of
human nature. As a movement it became known as Jansenism, named after a Belgian bishop and university professor who claimed it represented the thinking of the great
St. Augustine. According to the Jansenists original sin
utterly corrupted human nature making mankind incapable of goodness. The new pessimism held, contrary to the
spirit of the Enlightenment, that without the constant aid
of grace mankind was doomed not only to wickedness but
to wrong thinking. Most of mankind would be condemned
to hell through no fault of their own but simply because
grace was not available to them.

It was to the Catholic Church's credit that it recognized
this ready-made response to rationalism as destructive of
religion and condemned it. The Jesuits pleaded the Catholic case that men and women, without Jesus' saving grace,
were subject to temptation and death, yet were still capa-

ble of seeking justice and truth. To hold otherwise would be to capitulate to riotous irresponsibility. Salvation, it countered, was available to everyone and the means of grace were abundant within the church and its sacraments. Dour Jansenism nevertheless became almost a French national religion and was brilliantly expounded by Blaise Pascal. Although King Louis XIV and Pope Alexander VII combined to compel the rigorists to silence, the movement made the church in France resistant to papal influence for centuries. More insidiously, Jansenist misanthropy infected the French seminaries which trained priests of many nations, notably the Irish who became the backbone of the Catholic Church in the United States.

RIGIDITY AND REVOLUTION

Although it persisted in spiritual leadership throughout the eighteenth century, the papacy was dominated by the great Catholic rulers of France, Spain, and Austria, who routinely vetoed any papal candidate who showed signs of independence and initiative. In 1773, succumbing to political jealousy, Pope Clement XIV disbanded the entire Jesuit community. Jesuit effectiveness had waned, but the community retained worldwide influence and was devoted to the papacy. Nevertheless, to appease Europe's rulers Clement threw the leader of the Society of Jesus into prison where he died a miserable death, then dismantled six hundred religious houses and hundreds of schools, abandoning over twenty thousand priests and brothers.

As the Catholic Church became submissive to Europe's monarchs, it nevertheless associated with them and enjoyed privileges because of their patronage. But in 1789 the French Revolution introduced democracy into Europe and challenged papal authority by calling for direct election of the clergy in France. The Enlightenment had found political expression. When the new French democracy insisted that the clergy take an oath to uphold the new constitution, most bishops refused but half the priests agreed, protesting that King Louis XVI had done the same before he was executed.

As the rest of Europe turned against France, the holdouts among the clergy came to be considered traitors and the revolution took an ugly turn. The king was executed and the extremist Robespierre inaugurated a civil bloodbath. He introduced a new state religion, the Cult of Reason, which he hoped would appeal to Catholic and Protestant alike. It had but one teaching, man's immorality, and one commandment, to act responsibly. Some twenty thousand priests and bishops yielded to the revolution and abandoned their ministry. But the contrived Cult of Reason never appealed to the great mass of the French people and the attempt to take the eighty-one-year-old Pius VI into a new Avignon captivity failed when the old pope died on the journey. Realizing that, though he was master of Italy, he could not overcome the Christian faith of the

French, Napoleon told Cardinal Martiniana, "Go to Rome and tell the Holy Father that the First Consul wishes to make him a gift of 30 million Frenchmen."

POPES AND POLITICS

The price paid by the newly elected Pius VII for this "gift" was an agreement that allowed Napoleon to nominate bishops, retain church property confiscated by the revolution, and pay the clergy government salaries like civil servants. But when the pope refused to ally the Papal States with Napoleon's blockade of England, the emperor seized papal territory and the pope himself, whom he took to France for six years as prisoner, restoring him to Rome in 1814 only after his retreat from Russia presaged defeat for France. When Napoleon was defeated the Congress of Vienna in 1814 and 1815 restored the old order in Europe for a time, but it was to be a century of political revolution and church intransigence. Protestantism lacked political power. Where it was dominant it was contained politically in "national" churches such as those in Britain and Scandinavia. More congregational than international, Protestantism never aped the Catholic Church.

The popes of the nineteenth century possessed long memories and consistently resisted revolution, although the best Catholic thinkers urged the church to accommodate democratic movements in the belief that they were the best hope for human dignity and social justice as well as for religious toleration that would open Protestant nations to Catholic preaching.

When he was elected in 1846, Pius IX carried the reputation of a liberal and satisfied many by granting a constitution and limited democracy to the Papal States. But the widespread Revolution of 1848 in Europe forced the pope to flee Rome in disguise when his own citizens trained cannon on his residence. Pius was restored in 1850 only by French bayonets. From that point he became the intransigent foe of liberalism. Even when the Italian independence movement made him the virtual prisoner of the Vatican, he refused to negotiate.

By that time, however, Pius had raised the papacy to a new kind of power and influence not requiring territory. His thirty-two year reign was a virtuoso performance. Pius instituted audiences with common people and cultivated the common touch. But he also consolidated the papal right to teach and pronounce on what a Christian was expected to believe and do.

INFALLIBILITY

Throughout the Middle Ages it was assumed that church councils were infallible guides to Christian faith and morals. But Trent gave the impression that papal confirmation was required for conciliar decrees to have force. Now

Pius IX moved to call a council that would confirm the "coincidence of papal infallibility with the infallibility of the Church." To protests for moderation of this position the pope shouted, "Tradition! *I* am Tradition!" Sixty bishops deserted the First Vatican Council rather than have their votes counted publicly against the pope. The remaining 535 confirmed papal infallibility and were immediately dismissed by the pope in 1870. Having achieved this authority, Pius and his successors chose not to wield it, relying rather on persuasion.

Late in the century Leo XIII brought the moral influence of the Catholic Church behind demands for social justice in the new democracies. He championed the rights of collective bargaining and of the rising labor movement. Christian Democratic parties sprang up, notably in Italy and Germany, as Catholics began to involve themselves in elective politics. The first pope of the twentieth century, Pius X, was that rarity—a saint. His successor, Benedict XV, condemned both sides in the First World War and attempted in vain to play a role as peacemaker. He was excluded from the Versailles Peace Conference.

Rather than remain a virtual prisoner in the Vatican, Pius XI negotiated an agreement with Italy that gave the Catholic Church sovereignty in the tiny Vatican State in Rome. His successor, Pius XII, was elected on the eve of World War II. The new pope feared that peace would bring either a fascist or communist victory, so he steered a course of neutrality, surreptitiously aiding the Jews and managing a worldwide relief effort in the midst of hostilities. Pius quietly helped negotiate the Italian armistice and, in 1945, was chosen by Imperial Japan to mediate a peace short of unconditional surrender. The atomic bomb rendered the pope's role as peacemaker null.

By the middle of the twentieth century the papacy had exchanged political power for unparalleled moral influence. Yet, for all the popularity of Pius XII, he ruled the faithful as an autocrat with a theology and liturgy frozen since the Council of Trent four centuries earlier. His death in 1958, after a twenty-year reign, caught the church unprepared. The most likely successor, Archbishop Montini of Milan, was not yet a cardinal and the conclave was divided over whether the future of the church should be triumphalist or more democratic.

A NEW COUNCIL

As a compromise, and to buy time, the College of Cardinals chose the seventy-six-year-old patriarch of Venice, Angelo Roncalli, clearly intended to be a caretaker pope with a brief reign. As predicted, the new Pope John XXIII served briefly—only four and a half years—but in that time he initiated a revolution within the Catholic Church, meanwhile winning hearts around the world as perhaps the most winsome public figure of the twentieth century. By nature, John was democratic and unafraid. But he stunned the Christian world—Catholic and Protestant—when, in January 1959, he announced that he would summon the world's bishops to gather for an ecumenical council, the twenty-first in the church's history.

The Vatican bureaucracy protested that the church had no problems that the pope himself could not deal with, that a council was unpredictable, and that the church was already in the ascendancy. Pope John persisted, identifying the council as an inspiration of the Holy Spirit and offering a radical motive—his intention to reunite the churches and all Christians.

Vatican Council II opened in splendor on October 11, 1962, with 2,500 bishops in attendance, a number so diverse and unwieldy that the Vatican bureaucrats fully expected the conclave to approve recommendations of the commissions rather than attempt debate. But at the opening ceremonies the pope asserted a different agenda. John proclaimed an optimistic view of history, called for renewal of the church, and urged the bishops to take a pastoral rather than intellectual approach in presenting the church to the world.

As a direct consequence new commissions rejected all but one of the seventy draft documents the Curia had prepared for the council. Fortunately, the proposal for reform of the church's worship was acceptable in draft form for immediate consideration by the bishops, and a consensus was easily reached. Latin was replaced by the actual languages of the world's peoples, and the altar was ordered moved to face the people. Scripture readings, joint prayer and song, plus practical homilies enhanced corporate worship. Rites for the other sacraments were altered to revive early Christian symbolism and to stress the church's character as the family of God.

RECONCILIATION

At this peak of promise Pope John died. His passing was mourned throughout the world, notably by the many Protestant and Orthodox leaders he had invited to be official observers throughout the council. Shortly before John's death the Methodist observer Bishop Corson had asked the pope, "How long do you think it will be before Christian unity is realized—perhaps two hundred years?" The pope replied, "My dear Bishop Corson, you and I have achieved it already!"

Archbishop Montini of Milan had been Pope John's first cardinal and the old pope's protegé. He was easily elected at the age of sixty-five and took the name of Paul VI. He reopened the council, echoing John's agenda—renew the church, reunite Christendom, converse with the whole world.

The council itself benefited from religious liberty. For

the first time in history, a church council had been free to deliberate without the interference of secular governments. In simultaneous ceremonies in Rome and Constantinople, the Catholic and Orthodox Churches lifted the mutual excommunications that had divided them for nearly a millennium, moving a Protestant observer to comment: "If the Church is able to express its regret for the past with such ease and humility, anything is possible."

The church's understanding of itself had changed. Before the council, the Catholic Church was literally identified with the pope. Now it was understood as the people of God served by the clergy and by the bishops joined with the pope as bishop of Rome. Catholics were urged to pray and study with Protestants, and to collaborate in finding Christian solutions to social problems. Rather than exploit divergences with the churches of the Reformation, the council stressed the common heritage of all Christians and dedicated Catholicism to permanent reform. The church shed its nostalgia for the past. It acknowledged that, having lost political power of its own, the church enjoyed more freedom and moral influence than ever in history. The council placed the Catholic Church at the service of mankind and joined in a common quest to promote the dignity of man, welcoming all collaborators.

As in all revolutions, parties would form, enthusiasms would burn too brightly, idealism would turn to enmity, and many faithful would fall away when results fell short of promises. But these were the labor pains in bringing forth a new Catholic Christianity. Next we will look at Protestant Christianity with special reference to the American religious experience.

QUESTIONS FOR DISCUSSION AND SELF-STUDY

1. How did chivalry affect Christian culture?

2. What did new religious movements such as the Franciscans and Dominicans do to refresh the faith and reform the church?

3. What caused the crisis in the Catholic Church that led to the Reformation?

4. What did Martin Luther object to and what did he manage to change?

5. What did the Catholic Church do to reform itself?

CHAPTER 10

THE CHURCH AND REFORMATION

In the 1950s a well-publicized survey concluded that General Motors and the Catholic Church were the two best-managed organizations in the world. As I write this forty years later, GM has ousted its chief executive officer, closed factories, scheduled thousands of layoffs, and is deliberately downsizing itself.

The Catholic Church in the last decade of the twentieth century also looks less like a blue-chip corporation than it did in the mid-1950s. Declining church attendance, a steady exodus of priests and nuns, the clamor of gay believers for communion, the routine disregard of sanctions against contraception and abortion, and the forced closing of parochial schools all conspire to tarnish the well-oiled 1950s image of Holy Mother Church.

THE CHURCH AS PEOPLE OF GOD

However, while GM's stock has gone down, most Catholic Christians think the church is doing just fine, thank you, because they never fell for the corporate image in the first place. They know without prompting, as every Christian grasps, that the church is nothing more or less than the worldwide family of the baptized who worship with Christ principally in small community churches, who are of service to their communities and to one another, and who seek in common to follow the will of God. In the mid-1960s the Catholic Church called the Second Vatican Council to affirm, in part, that the church is the people of God. Protestant Christians never thought otherwise.

The pages of this book that cover the two millennia in the life of the church appear to give disproportionate attention to the Catholic Church. That is because it was identified as the Church of Christ in the West from at least the time of Constantine until Martin Luther—some twelve centuries—and because being a kind of monopoly forced it to be organized in such a monolithically institutional way. Those simple facts mean that it can be grasped and represented somewhat more easily than Protestantism which, because of its almost bewildering diversity, is much harder to describe.

The reluctant Christian must not only overcome his skepticism about but also his disinclination to join a church. For someone unaccustomed to common worship, a church community may appear confining. Who are these strangers? Why these rules and rituals? Why must I sing hymns and feign an earnestness and devotion I do not feel? Can't I pursue faith on my own?

The simple answer is no. Christianity is not a do-it-yourself religion and never has been. The members of God's family do not live private lives. Christ's command to love requires that we embrace both God and our fellow-man. That is done in the church and is exemplified in the local church community you will seek.

THE CHURCH AS SANCTUARY

The earliest Christians were inclined to gather together to protect themselves from a hostile world, to recreate the Last Supper of Jesus with his apostles, to refresh their memories of him, and to await his return. In Christian ages the church building itself has provided sanctuary for the hunted, the exiled, and the runaway. As I write, city churches through the United States are providing sanctuary for a new generation of the homeless, setting up cots in their lobbies, aisles, and basements.

Even as Christianity became the protected religion of empire and kings, it continued to be exemplified by small congregations in modest parish churches. Cathedrals were the spectacular skyscrapers of the Age of Faith; they were impressive but were also uncommon. Nearly all Christians worshipped in common with their neighbors in modest buildings as they do to this day.

Today, of course, a television evangelist can address more persons simultaneously in their homes than could gather in all the great cathedrals of the world combined. But it is not the same. The solitary Christian sitting before the television screen may gain inspiration and instruction, but the process in no way substitutes for worship and service in a church. The Baptist evangelist Billy Graham, a pioneer in television ministry, has always been careful to demonstrate no denominational bias in his preaching. Even more important, he has always insisted that his preaching is only an invitation to conversion, and that the Christian must find a church home to live out his or her faith.

CHRISTIANITY AND REFORM

The apparent fragmentation of the church into many denominations over the past four centuries is less an indictment of the traditional church than a sign of vitality in a Christian faith now two thousand years old. Catholics are inclined to characterize the Protestant Reformation as a revolt, but that is only because the Catholic Church was entrenched institutionally and politically and felt threatened by the dissenters.

In fact the Reformation was a reaffirmation of the original Gospel of God's graciousness as expounded by Jesus and St. Paul. It affirmed that man's good works do not earn him heaven. Rather, the Gospel is grace and good behavior is gratitude.

The old church had bitter experience over a millennium and a half with well-intentioned attempts to purify Christian faith and practice. It sanctioned some of these initiatives. The monastic movement, for example, was an attempt to recreate the spirit of the Christian communities of the first century. It was approved but then was forced to reform itself repeatedly as it lost its bearings and its innocence. The missionary movements of the Dark Ages and the mendicant friars of the Middle Ages were innovations sanctioned by the church as legitimate attempts—successful for a time—to restore the age of Peter and Paul and speed the conversion of the world to Christ. Religious orders sprang up in every century, each pursuing a special mission it felt had been neglected or given short shrift by the church. The church authorized these groups.

But for every successful attempt to refabricate the spirit of primitive Christianity, the Catholic Church was confronted with scores of reforms that carried the seeds of their own corruption. These it deemed heresies and it suppressed them. In retrospect we recognize heresies as radical attempts to reorganize the ideals of Christian living. Thus there were reformers who insisted that private property and marriage are seductive and therefore forbidden to true believers, that only perfect priests could dispense the sacraments, that only a penitential life could earn salvation. Typically, dissenting sects did not ask the church to be tolerant of them. They simply insisted that they were the true church.

RIGHTEOUSNESS AND ABSOLUTISM

In our own time of diversity and democracy it is difficult to sympathize with an institution that suppresses dissent, but the Catholic Church reasoned that erroneous beliefs and practices, however innocently preached, endangered the salvation of Christians. Protestant sects in their turn acted just as fanatically defensive and combative because they, like the Catholic establishment, believed that error in religion could be eternally dangerous to Christians.

The Catholic Church was also aware that reform movements were not composed simply of small bands of enthusiasts on the fringes of faith, but that these movements could supplant the church itself. When it became the faith of the Roman Empire in the fourth century, the Catholic Church claimed the adherence of only a large minority of Christians. The majority faith at the time was Arianism—a faith that, among other eccentricites, denied the divinity of Jesus.

Two analogies from our own time help to explain the Catholics' violent reaction to the reform movement that blossomed in the sixteenth century. In the 1940s and 1950s the House Un-American Activities Committee of the U.S. Congress confronted communist ideology as a threat to the Constitution and to the American way of life. Thus motivated, elected officials sought out and persecuted fellow Americans who had joined the communist movement in the Depression, many of whom were innocently seeking social reform and equal justice.

To our own day the U.S. Food & Drug Administration withholds new drugs from the market that might save Americans from suffering and death. The FDA's rationale is that the pharmaceutical manufacturers cannot be trusted to provide safe prescriptions. Drugs must be tested by the government to ensure that they do not have adverse effects. The process can and does take years, and many otherwise effective drugs are suppressed because of potentially dangerous side-effects. The very same protective mentality suffused the traditional church in the face of what we now know as the Reformation.

WHAT PROTESTANTISM CONFRONTED

To understand Protestantism we must see it as something other than a righteous reaction to a corrupt Catholic

Church. The church was not so much evil as it was complacent, ignorant, superstitious, and eccentric. In the early sixteenth century the church was not unlike the civil service of a sleepy banana republic—filled with petty bureaucrats and hangers-on with little sense of public service. Parish priests were poorly trained and often functionally illiterate. A mid-sixteenth-century survey of Gloucestershire found that 168 of 311 country clergy could not repeat the Ten Commandments and some professed ignorance of who authored The Lord's Prayer.

Moreover, priests in many places were largely unregulated in their conduct of worship and celebration of the sacraments. The very richness of the Christian faith had left simple believers prone to superstition, and mass credulity was common when the reform movement arose. The harshness of life on earth led common Christians of the time to fear the threat of eternal damnation, magnifying a fear that sometimes approached desperation. Jesus seemed distant and inaccessible; popular devotion leaned to the mother of Christ and to the saints. Before the invention of printing the Bible was available in rare handwritten copies only, so there was little either layman or priest could rely on to rectify superstition.

What is striking about the emergence of Protestantism is that the officialdom within the Catholic Church had become complacent, but individual Christians never cared more deeply about religion—if only for fear of damnation. Martin Luther, the first great figure of the Reformation, is a perfect example of reform that stemmed from personal desperation for the way of salvation. As a young man fearing for his life in a thunderstorm, he cried out a desperate prayer: "Help me, St. Anne, and I will become a monk." It was not only death Luther feared, but his uncertainty of salvation, an anxiety common to Christians of the time that was not satisfied by a church that dispensed rites and indulgences. The consciences of Christians were not comforted by externals.

Even a cursory examination of the sixteenth century illustrates how readily the church reformed itself during the lifetime of Luther, Calvin, and its principal critics. The Council of Trent in midcentury imposed a discipline on the Catholic Church that curbed moral excesses of the clergy, set standards for training and worship, clarified the articles of faith, and suppressed superstition. But in retrospect it becomes abundantly clear that Luther and the other reformers had something else altogether in mind than having the Catholic Church clean up its act. They did not seek merely to reform an existing institution but to redefine—and even recreate—the very character of the church.

RECREATING THE CHURCH

It is striking to note how readily the followers of the early reformers shrugged off religious habits that had been ingrained for centuries in Christian practice. It was routine in the late Middle Ages for Christians to provide for their happy death by a lifelong regimen of "good works" which included charitable practices and philanthropy, but more accurately consisted of piling up prayers and religious observances, stocking a treasury of grace that might be weighed against one's sins by God at the end of one's life and thus earn salvation.

The pursuit of good works failed to relieve the anxiety of Christians with regard to their salvation. Luther and the other reformers concluded that the effort was pointless, and the first Protestant Christians dropped them with abandon. To learn that a lifelong investment in time and money to earn an uncertain salvation is futile was, in a sense, a relief. Luther joked about his own frenetic pursuit of good works as a young man. "If ever a monk got to heaven through monkery," he insisted, "I would have been that man."

But anxiety remained. If not by works, how could one gain salvation? Through faith, Luther insisted, and laid the foundations of Protestant Christianity wherein man is not justified through his moral effort but through the loving mercy of Jesus. Faith is not just intellectual assent to a creed but a total personal commitment of the self to God. But the Christian does not even generate his own faith. Rather, faith is a gift from God to be accepted. The faithful Christian must do good but not for reward. Rather, man's good deeds are only an expression of his faith and freedom. Faith comes not from doing but from hearing the word of God as contained in the Bible.

The implications of this approach were devastating to the institutional church. If the Christian is justified by faith, there is no need for priests and no real distinction between clergy and ordinary Christians. Monasticism is no longer a higher vocation than that of the ordinary believer, nor is celibacy the key to a higher reward. Rather, every man and woman is minister to every other. The sacraments might be retained in some form but clearly subordinated to the word contained in Scripture. Man's conscience, liberated by faith, is supreme. The institutional church is now only the visible assembly of faithful individuals who worship together and minister to one another. The age of soaring cathedrals is over, replaced by individual worshippers.

ANARCHY AND DISCIPLINE

The reformers were not unaware that this liberating approach to Christianity was an implicit invitation to anarchy. If each man's conscience is pope, then there are as many churches as Christians. The reformers insisted that good works cannot alter the essential imperfection of man, but some discipline is necessary for men and women of faith. The eccentricities of individual conscience cannot guarantee order.

Accordingly, secular rulers stepped in not only to protect reform movements within their territories but to ensure discipline and lawfulness. When Henry VIII broke from the papacy, he ensured that the Church of England would be both Catholic and reformed. As a consequence, Anglicanism neither denigrates nor diminishes the Word or the Sacrament of God since both convey the Gospel and both are means of grace.

Following England's example it became the practice in predominantly Protestant lands, such as Scandinavia, to create national churches. The word "Protestant," incidentally, refers to the early refusal of reformers to contain the movement within geographical borders. By 1600 reformed churches extended throughout England and Europe south to the Spanish border and as far east as Hungary.

The quickness of secular governments to protect, discipline, and—in many cases—to institutionalize the Protestant churches within their borders put a damper on the spirit of reform and tended to create new and rigid orthodoxies as onerous as the Catholic Church. Dissident movements emerged as faith and conscience created new ways of worshipping God, proclaiming Christ, and seeking salvation. Thus the Puritans, the Anabaptists, the Methodists, and the Quakers became alternative reform movements within nations with "official" Protestant faiths.

THE AMERICAN EXPERIENCE

Nowhere was the proliferation and diversity of faiths more apparent than in America. The early attempt to establish monopolies of Puritans in New England, Quakers in Pennsylvania, Catholics in Maryland, and Anglicans elsewhere quickly broke down as the frontier offered freedom and successive waves of migrants kept changing the mix. In America religion did not need the protection of the state; it flourished and diversified on its own.

The separation of church and state in the new nation was presaged by the charter given by Charles II of England to William Penn. It provided that no one "at any time be compelled to frequent or maintain any religious worship, place or ministry whatever contrary to his or her mind." In 1749 Benjamin Franklin called for the creation of a distinctively Christian "public religion" that might ensure civility in the nation soon to be born, but he was ignored. An official religion was not needed.

Their diversity of faiths, however, did not detract from the common belief of Americans in a manifest destiny— that this is God's country. The U.S. government provides tax relief for churches to this day, but the practice is viewed not so much as favoring religion as protecting it from interference by the secular state.

The big three denominations of colonial America— Congregational, Presbyterian, and Episcopal—were displaced by Baptists, Methodists, and Disciples of Christ as the frontier was pushed back. Utopianism and revivalism have nourished Christianity in America and sanctioned its further proliferation into new denominations inconceivable to the sixteenth-century reformers—Shakers, Latter Day Saints, Christian Scientists, Seventh Day Adventists, and Jehovah's Witnesses among them. Not to be outdone, the Catholic Church has been thoroughly accepted as an American institution, claiming more adherents than any single Protestant denomination.

Today the typical American small town literally has a house of worship on every downtown corner, and the churches—whatever their denomination—play an important role in the community beyond Sunday worship. During the week they provide a home for Boy Scouts and Girl Scouts, Alcoholics Anonymous, child care, women's support groups, drug rehabilitation, and a range of ministries that have no denominational stamp but serve to bind Americans together as a caring society. Despite (or perhaps because of) its more than two hundred denominations, the church in the United States has reinvented itself and prepares confidently to enter the Third Millennium of the Christian faith.

QUESTIONS FOR DISCUSSION AND SELF-STUDY:

1. How do Christians reconcile their one faith with their division into many denominations?

2. Can all churches legitimately claim to be expressions of one church?

3. What did the Reformation actually reform and what did it produce that was new?

4. What is unique about Christianity in America?

5. In what respects is the church more than a club for Christians?

CHAPTER 11

UNPOPULAR MESSAGES AND UNSOLVED MYSTERIES

Any attempt to explain Christianity would be incomplete without confronting the "hard sayings" of Jesus and the riddles of faith that remain after even the closest reading of the Bible. Christian belief is neither simply stated nor easily practiced. If mankind and the world merited the Son of God becoming a man and dying for us on a cross, we should not be surprised that there is a dark and unresolved side to humanity that needs to be acknowledged by the reluctant Christian.

ORIGINAL SIN

Humanists, who insist that mankind is the measure of all things in the universe, are offended by any intimation that men and women might carry inherent flaws. They reason that if society is perfectible then human beings (the raw material of society) must be inherently good.

Christians agree that people are capable of improving. Jesus was not indulging in hyperbole when he told his followers to "be perfect, as my heavenly Father is perfect." But Christians also acknowledge the universal experience that all men and women lack natural integrity, reliability, and good will. As St. Paul and St. Augustine eloquently testified, human flesh and the human spirit are often at odds. Paul, reflecting on his own behavior, admitted that often "the good that I would I do not: but the evil that I would not, that I do." Augustine, struggling to reconcile his devotion to God with his sensuality, prayed: "Give me chastity, but not yet!"

We are not the people we want to be and know we ought to be. Rather than acting on our best instincts, we rationalize our behavior that falls short of ideal as "only human." Innocence is elusive at any age. No one who has reflected on the natural cruelty of children can blame it simply on their corruption by adults. We are at odds with ourselves and others from the first bawling complaints we utter as we emerge from the womb. Accordingly, if we seek to be perfect, as Jesus commands, it is only through God's grace that we can bring order from our own inner chaos and remedy our shortcomings. We cannot reclaim an innocence we never possessed, but we can ask God for integrity.

Original sin is the name that describes what we experience in ourselves and all others—a disjunction between intellect, will, and senses—which in extreme forms is found in our prisons and mental hospitals. This basic condition is simply a fact of life; we did not cause it in ourselves, but we are responsible to seek and accept the grace to heal this fundamental crack in our character. The mission of science and technology can be read as an attempt to improve on physical nature—eventually to recreate Eden. Improving human nature, however, is a task beyond the pretensions of scientists and engineers. Although social behavior can be modified for the better, human nature requires redemption.

At the very beginning of the Bible original sin appears in the story of Adam and Eve, our first parents, who were placed by God in a perfect world. Yet senselessly they rebelled against the God who made them, creating a breach with him that exposed cracks within their personalities. Christians disagree whether the story of our first parents is all allegory or based on fact, but it is certain that original sin did not consist of eating an apple nor did it have anything to do with sex. What is clear from the story is that the first human beings rejected their dependent relationship with their Creator. The allure of the "forbidden fruit" in the story was that it held the promise of releasing them from their dependence on God and turning them into gods themselves.

The original sin was a generic choice of self over God—

a pretentious declaration of independence. What it accomplished was to expose further the lack of integrity in our first parents and their utter state of dependency. The shame that caused Adam and Eve to cover their nakedness is a reflection of the contradictory passions they felt and could no longer control by themselves. In presuming to proclaim their independence from God they condemned themselves to their own inner frailties.

The story of redemption that forms the underlying plot of the Bible traces God's attempts to mend the original breach and restore integrity. That story led, of course, to God's Son suffering for sin and dying for love of every individual. Why such a drastic solution on God's part was required to save us from ourselves remains a mystery. Equally elusive is identifying precisely what God's redeeming grace has done to restore our lost wholeness. After Jesus' total sacrifice we are still aware of the contradiction and fragmentation in our nature. But we have God's word that Jesus' obedience unto death mended the break. Now, by baptism, we are graced and joined to Christ. We still struggle, but we are clearly called to perfection and we are capable of being restored to God.

HELLFIRE AND PREDESTINATION

Christian revelation makes it evident that there is both a heaven and a hell, salvation and damnation. Dante's allegory of the afterlife haunts our imaginations, repelling and frightening us. The *Divine Comedy* is one comedy that does not inspire laughter. Why would a good God want to punish us, whatever our offenses?

The answer is that we are the architects of our own damnation. We condemn ourselves by reaffirming the original sin—choosing ourselves, worshipping our own independence. All we know about hell is that it is an eternity with ourselves and without God. Even if we dismiss hellfire as metaphor, hell consists of stewing in our own juices. Damnation is not accidental; it is chosen. It is the consequence of rejecting God—a divorce initiated by creatures against their Creator. In his play *No Exit* Jean-Paul Sartre depicted hell as a locked room inhabited by self-absorbed people condemned eternally to live in one another's neurotic company. One of the philosopher-playwright's characters complains that "Hell is other people." Sartre makes it clear, however, that the most damnable aspect of hell is being condemned to live eternally with oneself.

Some Christians as they reflect on sin as the rejection of God by his creatures conclude that every person is predestined to either salvation or damnation. It is true that an all-seeing God can predict whether we will reject him in the end, but he neither causes the rejection nor does the rejecting. For all any person knows, we will all be saved because God somehow is able to break through our self-preoccupation with his mercy. But I, for one, wouldn't bet on it.

In the New Testament the rejection of God was exemplified most dramatically in the betrayal of Jesus by the apostle Judas, one of his closest friends, for thirty pieces of silver. Jesus, aware of Judas' coming treachery, reflected that "it would have been better for this man had he never been born." Later, Judas despaired at his having handed Jesus over to his death and hanged himself. Are we to assume that Judas was predestined from the womb to damnation? Clearly not, for it would have been hypocritical of Jesus to have taken him on as an apostle in the first instance.

If Judas indeed was condemned (which only God knows), it was not by his treachery but by his refusal to seek forgiveness. Judas' only "unforgivable sin" could have been giving in to despair and taking his own life. Although God's mercy is endless it can be rejected. We are all aware of times we prefer perversely to be wrong than to be sorry. If mercy were forced on mankind, we would lose our freedom and thereby our distinction among creatures. Compliant puppets do not need God's mercy. Our ability to choose is what being created in God's image means.

The more responsible and loving we are in life, the more sensitive we are to God, and therefore the closer to heaven, which is the state of being in God's presence. On the other hand, the more we wallow in self and indifference or cause pain and separation, the more we isolate ourselves and construct a lonely hell on earth that presages an eternity of isolation. God's mercy is ineffective unless we accept it. Ironically, those who most need forgiveness are those least inclined to believe they need it.

Jesus' call to repentance is his constant invitation to avail ourselves of God's mercy. Righteousness for the Christian is not the smug self-satisfaction of the religious rulekeeper; rather it is the humble disposition of men and women who are aware of their flaws but whose lives are turned toward mercy and love. Conversion literally means "turning around" from the direction one is going in order to face God. Conversion is the daily task of every Christian.

SATAN

If Jesus is good incarnate, the devil is evil personified. Ironically, Satan is routinely dismissed because he is so imaginatively depicted in our literature and films and television. Drama thrives on conflict, and villains are more interesting than heroes. Satan makes the best villain because his powers to harm us are supernatural. Dostoevski said of the devil, "If [Satan] doesn't exist, but man has created him, he has created him in his own image and likeness."

Earlier ages took the devil more seriously than we do, not because they were more inclined to superstition, but because they were more aware of evil as a fact and a force in human affairs. In our own times we incline to rationalize evil as accident or inadvertence and we tend to interpret evil intention as little more than the sick thinking of misguided persons.

However inconvenient and unsophisticated, the existence of an evil spirit is clear in revelation. Satan is present at the beginning of the Old Testament, providing the motivation for the original sin of our first parents. He returns in the New Testament to tempt Jesus himself to be only human—first offering the world to the Son of God, then, at the end, tempting Jesus to avoid the cross altogether under the impression he had been abandoned by his Father.

The reluctant Christian will not find it any harder to believe in evil personified than in a personal God. Evil is anything but an abstraction. When the Apostle Peter grabbed Jesus and rebuked him for predicting his imminent suffering and death, Jesus turned on his friend in fury: "Get behind me, Satan! You are a hindrance to me; for you are not on the side of God, but of men."

Satan is sinister, not quaint. Forget the fiery eyes, scales, and pointed tail. Satan is an angel, a spirit created by God, who rebelled against his Creator before Adam and Eve. He is neither misguided nor does he pursue evil for pleasure. He acts through hatred and seeks our destruction. Jesus did not become human and suffer and die to give us an example of good manners, but to redeem us from evil. It is Jesus' conquest of evil that renders Satan powerless to harm those who accept redemption and love God.

HEAVEN

One of the attractions of Islam is its depiction of heaven as the perfect recreation of the original Eden. Each faithful follower of the Prophet can conceive of heaven as the fulfillment of all his or her earthly aspirations. In contrast, the Christian conception of heaven is less that of a pleasure palace than of the fulfillment that comes from rejoining the creature with its Creator. Heaven for the Christian is as indescribable as a love affair. When I was younger I was dismayed by how many Christian prayers refer to heaven as "eternal rest" because an eternity of just lying around didn't seem attractive to me. Now that I am older, busier, and often deprived of sleep, the prospect of a restful eternity is much more attractive.

Heaven is being with God as our personal fulfillment. Only the Creator knows ultimately what will satisfy the creature. Accordingly, theologians are reluctant to speculate much about the afterlife. Heaven is a relationship that already exists but of which we are only imperfectly aware. When we are face to face with God the relationship will be complete. We do know, however, that heaven, like earthly love, is not just "spiritual." The central event of the Christian faith is the Resurrection. When Jesus triumphed over death, opening the way for us to follow him, he did not rise as some disembodied soul freed of its body. Jesus was restored to life whole, both in body and spirit. After the

Resurrection the doubting Apostle Thomas satisfied himself that the risen Christ was no ghost.

Accordingly Christians have shown great respect for the bodies of the dead, preferring burial to cremation. The dignity and hopefulness in Christian funerals is not a product of superstition but rather an acknowledgement that we will somehow be whole again in heaven—not angels but human. So perhaps, after all, there is an element of the Islamic paradise in the Christian heaven.

MIRACLES

Miracles are expressions of God's intervention in the normal course of things to make something special happen. Usually a miracle is a suspension of natural processes or (as we used to call them) the laws of nature and is meant to improve on them. Jesus worked miracles in his lifetime by bringing his friend Lazarus back to life, feeding hungry multitudes, curing the sick, restoring sight and limbs, and much more. Some of his miracles seem almost frivolous—walking on water, and turning water into wine for a wedding reception.

Not so many years ago miracles were objected to because they seemed to demonstrate that God didn't get things right in the first place. Scientists like an orderly, predictable universe even when it displays destructive tendencies. Technology, of course, aims at improving on nature, but to do that we need to know what nature is up to. When God intervenes, some scientists contend, he is no longer playing by rules of his own creation.

We now realize that nature's "laws" are at least as complicated as the civil and criminal code contained in all those dense volumes we see in lawyers' offices. Accordingly, though we may pray for miracles, we cannot be certain that the remission of cancer or restoration of sight or hearing indicates a divine intervention or just a rare but natural occurrence.

What we do know is that Jesus was reluctant to work miracles because he did not wish to attract his followers to faith by showmanship. He also did not work miracles for his own benefit. His life was hard and his death a horror. He did nothing to improve his own comfort.

We also know that many of the disasters in life are not caused by evil intent but by accident or by the ineluctable sweep of natural forces. Cancer, however dreadful, is not malevolent. It grows and destroys by some dumb inner imperative. Hurricanes and floods wreak their destruction not by malice but by their nature. If God employed miracles to bail us out of all trouble he would be reinventing the universe at every moment.

In extreme situations Christians nevertheless call on God for assistance, but they are not overly disappointed when a miracle is not forthcoming. The freedom of the sons and daughters of God depends on the Creator refraining from tinkering constantly with his handiwork.

PUTTING A CAMEL THROUGH THE
EYE OF A NEEDLE

Jesus was a storyteller, and his stories typically take the form of parables, each with a moral. Faith, for example, could be compared with a mustard seed—a mere speck with the potential of growing into something grand. God could be compared to a lord who deals evenhandedly with his servants but rewards those who make the most of his investments in them. The kingdom of heaven could be compared with a wedding banquet many of whose guests ignore the invitation, so the host invites everyone he can find but expects even these strangers to be "dressed" properly for the occasion.

Effective as these stories are, they are not as clear as, say, the Ten Commandments or even Jesus' own prescriptions for the good life contained in the Sermon on the Mount. It is our own contemporary fashion to be literal and unpoetic and to wish that the authors of the Gospels would have written more like journalists, giving us God's revelation in terms of who, what, where, when, and how.

Jesus apparently did not feel constrained to preach like a journalist, scientist, or lawyer, so biblical scholars have kept busy for twenty centuries attempting to determine with greater accuracy and comprehensiveness what Jesus meant by what he said and what he would have said about issues he frankly chose not to address fully or at all.

The reluctant Christian is typically more tolerant of Jesus' ambiguity than of his clarity. You can probably get along with being uncertain how Jesus stands on the topic of capital punishment or immigration or income distribution, but you may feel uncomfortable when he speaks bluntly and clearly. I do.

Does Jesus really mean what he is saying when he states that it is easier for a camel to pass through the eye of a needle than for a rich person to gain heaven? Is he serious that a man should pluck out his eye rather than look at a woman with lust? Did he really mean that divorce was deserving of punishment and that we must love our enemies?

These are the parts of the Bible that make us squirm and that confirm our reluctance as Christians. We cannot ignore them altogether nor can we attribute them all to Middle Eastern hyperbole and colorful speech. Jesus would not have addressed these topics if he had not considered them important. His language may be more graphic than we would like, but it is clear that he is making a point and that he has expectations of Christians that we would rather not have of ourselves.

The apparent incompatibility of personal wealth with salvation has led Christians for the past two millennia to give generously to charity during their lifetimes and to ensure that excess wealth go to good causes once they die. Ironically, the wealth that helped to weaken the medieval church came from generations of wealthy believers who endowed it rather than suffer the fate of camels attempting to pass through the eyes of needles.

If you have not met many one-eyed Christians it is not because Jesus' followers have not felt the occasional stirring of lust nor is it because they are hypocrites who ignore their Savior. Jesus asks much more of us than most of us can consistently provide. In a sense there is no such thing as a "good" Christian, for even the best of the saints fell short and we are called to perfection. But there are a lot of faithful Christians—those who acknowledge their shortcomings, who ask for and accept forgiveness, and who attempt to live by the single rule of love. You can be one of them.

QUESTIONS FOR DISCUSSION AND SELF-STUDY:

1. What do you find hardest to believe about the Christian faith?

2. Does Jesus command anything that you consider impossible or unreasonable?

3. What is hell? What is heaven? Who is Satan?

4. What is the nature of evil?

5. How do you deal with Jesus' command to love your enemies? To turn the other cheek? To prefer poverty to wealth? To suppress desire?

CHAPTER 12

ONE CHURCH, MANY CHOICES

A SUPERMARKET OF WORSHIP

Although nearly half of all Americans worship regularly, they do so through a bewilderingly diverse number of denominations. Even the smallest town can offer its resident half-a-dozen or more traditional ("mainstream") Protestant denominations plus a Catholic parish and an assortment of Evangelical churches and assemblies. Why so many? Why are they so different? And why can't they get together and agree?

Religious diversity in the United States stems from at least three sources: immigration, revivalism, and what might be termed an American tradition of self-reliance. We are a nation of immigrants. Settlers brought their denominations with them and they are still here, transplanted and Americanized. The challenge of the frontier joined to native idealism and individualism fostered even more denominations. Dissidents formed splinter churches following the perennial compulsion to resurrect the authentic faith and life of the Christian community in the apostolic age.

In one sense this diversity is dismaying because it contradicts Christ's prayer that we "all may be one" as Jesus and his Father are joined. Yet diversity does not appear to have weakened the church in America; instead it seems to be a sign of vitality. By contrast some nations with legally established churches seem to be prone to complacency, with churchgoing the exception rather than the rule. In the United States, for whatever reason, diversity seems to nourish faith and worship.

Moreover, diversity prompts the many Christian denominations to find ways to cooperate to accomplish common goals. In nearly every American community clergy of many denominations are linked in interfaith fellowships and their congregations pool resources to address problems beyond the parish community—AIDS, homelessness, aging, disaster relief, child care, addiction, and more. Regardless of denominational affiliation, local churches open their facilities to community needs without asking the affiliation of those they serve. The local Boy Scout troop may meet at the Catholic church, while the Campfire Girls gather at the Methodist parish, and Alcoholics Anonymous finds space at the Baptist church down the road. By far the greatest source of philanthropy in the United States consists of contributions made by individual

Americans to their churches, but much of that money is spent on needs of the society at large. In 1991 Americans gave $39.2 billion to their churches to do good; $6.6 billion of it was redirected to other organizations and individuals serving social needs unrelated to religion. In addition, in 1991 43 percent of American churchgoers' volunteer time (with an estimated value of $19.2 billion) was applied to church-sponsored service to the secular community.

FINDING A CHURCH HOME

I grew up in a small suburb of Chicago where the prominent evangelist Billy Graham began his ministry at a local church. Mr. Graham comes from the Baptist tradition and was trained at Wheaton College not far away. But Graham's ministry has never been narrowly denominational. Before his "crusades" enter an American city he contacts local clergy of many denominations to ensure that they will provide a permanent church home to nourish the new faith of his converts. Without follow-up and mutual concern, faith is fragile. Christianity does not thrive in private nor can faith be sustained by emotional fervor alone. Christians new and old need to find the support and the challenge of a community. That means joining a local church.

How is the reluctant Christian to choose among so many alternatives? In the balance of this chapter I will describe something about the major denominations, each of which has a singular character and fervor, a spareness or complexity, a moral strictness or latitude, sophistication or informality. Each also has a theology that does not completely accord with others, so we need to dismiss out of hand any notion that the major differences among the churches can be reduced to mere style or fashion.

On the other hand, it would be false to suggest that American churches wear their differences on their sleeves. One Sunday years ago when I was editor of a large community newspaper in Connecticut, I assigned staff to services in the town's churches so we could compare notes on the messages being delivered from a dozen pulpits. As expected, the preaching varied in quality and the demands it put on its hearers, but the subjects and contents of the sermons were virtually interchangeable. The Presbyterians were not preaching predestination that day. Catholics were not arguing clerical celibacy or papal infallibility. Lutherans were not being reminded of their founder's theses challenging the medieval church, and no sermon was critical of any other denomination. Rather, the Gospel of God's saving love and mankind's mutual responsibility were common themes with many variations. The messages were not bland, but neither were they divisive or contentious.

As I write, one of our daughters is "shopping" for a

church in the small city where she recently settled as a young, single woman attending graduate school. I hope that she settles on a church home in the tradition in which she was raised, but I know she brings needs to any Christian congregation that she did not have as a child. She is looking for companions her own age in a young adult group, sermons that speak to a woman living on her own, and opportunities to be of service to the disadvantaged. I do not believe my daughter is a traitor to her own tradition by looking for a church family—of whatever denomination—that matches her current situation and helps her grow in the knowledge and love of God and in service to others.

Many reluctant Christians return to churchgoing not because of a surge in their own faith but because they now have young children and realize church membership strengthens the family. There is no hypocrisy in joining a congregation for mixed reasons. It is the function of the church family to strengthen the faith and love of members, not to assume they are fully mature.

ROMAN CATHOLIC

Since the Second Vatican Council in the 1960s Catholic worship has lost much of the exotic character that made a Catholic Mass appear so dramatically different from Protestant services. The Latin language gave way to the vernacular and Catholics have long since shared many hymns with Protestants, preferring simple congregational singing to performing Palestrina. Often Catholics at worship will sing folk tunes to a guitar rather than to organ accompaniment.

Nevertheless, Catholic worship remains largely fixed and traditional. The Mass is not simply a prayer service but rather a symbolic reenactment of Jesus' life, death, and Resurrection. Catholics believe that Christ is truly present and that the Holy Spirit makes their worship effective. The term "Mass" has been largely replaced by "Eucharist," meaning thanksgiving. In the course of this ancient rite Catholics repent of their sins, Jesus becomes present under the forms of bread and wine (as at the Last Supper) and is shared as Communion with the faithful.

Catholics believe in corporate worship because they define the church as the mystical body of Christ of which each Christian is a functioning member. Catholic clergy refer to themselves as both priests and ministers—priests because they reenact Christ's sacrifice, ministers because they serve God's people. In addition to the Eucharist, Catholics believe that God works through the church to grace his people through six other sacraments—Baptism, Penance or Reconciliation, Confirmation, Holy Orders (ordination), Matrimony, and the Anointing of the Sick. Catholics confess their sins collectively (without detail) and privately to a priest.

By dint of where they live, Catholics are assigned to a local parish with geographic boundaries, although they can apply for good reason to transfer to another parish. Since Catholics are so numerous and are expected to worship every Saturday or Sunday plus major feast days, the typical Catholic church schedules many services to accommodate them.

Although preaching is increasingly emphasized in Catholic churches, the sermon is not as central as in Protestant churches and is sometimes replaced by a brief homily. The Word of God is incorporated with the Sacrifice of the Mass and the sacramental action of the Eucharist. Whereas Protestant sermons average twenty minutes or more, Catholic preaching is often only half as long, or less, and the Catholic Sunday service altogether runs about an hour whereas a Protestant service is typically half again or twice as long.

ORTHODOX

Orthodoxy represents a separation of the Eastern Church from Western Catholicism that dates to the twelfth century. Unlike the Protestant revolt of the sixteenth century, Orthodoxy did not take issue with major Catholic doctrine and practice but rather with authority and discipline. For example, Orthodoxy does not recognize the pope's authority in the East and its clergy have the option of marrying.

Because of Orthodoxy's Eastern roots it is, for cultural reasons more than any other, still considered an exotic faith in the United States. Orthodox worship, like that of Catholicism, is sacramental and richly ritualistic. The approximately four hundred parishes of the Orthodox Church in America now employ mostly English in their rites, but the Greek Archdiocese and the Ukrainian Orthodox Church continue to reflect their ethnic roots. Total Orthodox membership in America is estimated at more than 3 million. The Orthodox Church in America is a member of both the National and World Council of Churches.

As religious freedom in Russia revives the ancient faith in its homeland after more than seventy years of Soviet suppression, more attention will focus on Orthodoxy as a vital Christian presence in the United States.

BAPTIST

As an English-speaking denomination, Baptists originated within seventeenth-century Puritanism. The strain that developed most successfully in the United States was strongly Calvinist—maintaining that Christ died for the elect—but also ecumenical in spirit, seeking bonds of unity with other Christians. Baptists do not demand an all-

embracing denominational structure; most keep to auton-
omously governed local congregations. The core doctrine
that gives them their name is the insistence that Baptism
is reserved for adult believers alone contrary to the
centuries-old tradition of infant Baptism. Total bodily im-
mersion in water is considered by Baptists to be a more apt
symbol of rebirth in Christ than traditional pouring or
sprinkling.

Early Baptist churches in America were mostly indige-
nous rather than transplanted from Britain and continental
Europe. The first Baptist church was established in Providence, Rhode Island, by Roger Williams in 1639 after his
expulsion from the Massachusetts Bay Colony. Although
seemingly restricted by its insistence on Baptism of the
elect alone, the Baptist faith thrived during the eighteenth
century, when many Christians announced themselves
"awakened" by revivalist preaching and sought to be born
again of water and the Spirit. In the two decades after 1775
the number of Baptist congregations increased from 494 to
1,152. After the Civil War former slaves formed their own
Baptist churches, and in 1880 the black National Convention was formed, to which the National Baptist Convention, USA was added in 1916.

By 1900 Baptists had largely dispensed with Calvinist
rigidity in favor of evangelicalism and a religion of the
"heart," but the movement still retained an interest in
theology. All Baptists hold to six common convictions: (1)
the supreme authority of the Bible over any creed, (2)

Baptism for adult believers alone, (3) a church composed solely of believers who give clear evidence of their faith, (4) equality of all Christians in the church and responsibility for all to minister to one another, (5) the independence and autonomy of each local congregation, and (6) separation of church and state.

Baptist worship often consists of exposition of scriptural revelation in a sermon together with extemporaneous prayers and congregational hymn singing. Communion is received in the pews rather than at an altar or table and is observed monthly rather than weekly.

CONGREGATIONAL (UNITED CHURCH)

Congregationalists trace their origins to churches formed in England in the late sixteenth and seventeenth centuries when they were often known as Independents. Congregationalists place great emphasis on the autonomy of each local assembly. In the United States they are an outgrowth of both the Separatists of the Plymouth Colony and the Puritans of the Massachusetts Bay Colony. It was Congregationalists who founded Harvard in 1639 to ensure a trained Christian ministry. With the Great Awakening that began in 1734 many Congregationalists in New England revived their strict Calvinist traditions while others moved into a noncreedal Unitarianism. But as the nation moved westward in the nineteenth century, Congregationalism moved with it and thrived, often in association with Presbyterians. Between the two World Wars Congregationalists merged with the Christian Church, then in 1961 united with the Evangelical and Reformed Church to form the United Church of Christ.

Contemporary Congregationalists share some of the outlook of evangelical Protestants with an emphasis on free movement of the Spirit in each congregation and an aversion to creeds. The primitive confession of faith, "Jesus is Lord," is normally sufficient basis for membership. Preaching is central to Congregational worship because the Word of God in Scripture is considered to constitute the church. Baptism of infants by sprinkling is practiced, and the Lord's Supper is celebrated once or twice a month. Congregationalists believe that it is the Spirit of God that "gathers" them into the local church community.

EPISCOPAL

The Anglican community is one of three major movements that broke with the papacy in the sixteenth century—the others being Lutherans and the Reformed (Calvinist) churches. The Church of England broke with the pope during the reign of Henry VIII but, it insisted, not with the Catholic faith.

In its American incarnation at the time of the War of Independence the Anglican faith in the colonies became known as the Protestant Episcopal Church. For this reason I have included it as a Protestant faith. However, the Anglican worldwide communion of twenty-three independent national churches exhibits a great latitude between Catholic and Protestant doctrine and practice. Indeed, Anglicanism has been called the "middle way" of "reformed Catholicism"—namely a church reformed in worship and custom but Catholic in teaching and practice.

The Episcopal Church holds to the Catholic faith of the Scriptures and the early church fathers. It acknowledges the authority of civil government but does not submit to it, respecting the freedom of the individual. As its name implies, the Episcopal Church traces the authority of its bishops to the apostles. It strives to maintain a balance between the Word of God and the sacramental action of God's Spirit in the church. Episcopal clergy function as both priests and ministers but often eschew the title "Father." Episcopal parishes are governed by lay vestries elected by all parish members.

The archbishop of Canterbury is not only chief pastor of his diocese and over the Church of England (through its synods and convocations), but he is respected and revered throughout the Anglican community and his words carry great moral authority if not worldwide jurisdiction.

While its ritual is rich, the Episcopal Church recognizes as strictly sacramental only those rites—Eucharist and

Baptism—clearly instituted by Jesus. Episcopal worship is outlined in the Book of Common Prayer, a work of literary merit as well as piety, which includes rites, prayers, and scriptural readings. A typical Episcopal service consists of either celebration of the Eucharist or the recitation of Morning Prayer, consisting largely of psalms, Bible readings, hymns, and sermons and derived from ancient monastic prayer. In architecture and furnishings Episcopal churches often include rich symbolism.

L U T H E R A N

Although the Lutheran Church dates from the Augsburg Confession of 1530, application of the reformer's name to it was avoided until the seventeenth century, with theologians preferring to designate it as the "apostolic Catholic church" or "Catholic evangelical church." The official teaching of the Lutheran Church is contained in the Book of Concord of 1580.

Martin Luther held that Christians "are justified freely on account of Christ through faith when they believe that they are received into grace and their sins forgiven on account of Christ, who by his death made satisfaction for our sins." In other words, the faithful acknowledge they are accepted by God in spite of their unacceptability.

The Bible contains law and promises. Since mankind is incapable of being inwardly and outwardly obedient to

God's will, we are driven to despondency, but God's promise conquers despair by justifying the unjust. Luther restricted predestination to salvation for believers but withheld imputing certain damnation to unbelievers.

The reformer did not trace his church to institutional Catholicism. Rather, he defined the church as the "congregation of saints [believers] in which the gospel is purely taught and the sacraments rightly administered." By "gospel" he meant that Christ justifies through individual faith rather than merit. Luther judged the church to be as weak and sinful as any other organization, but he affirmed that God works through it nonetheless because it is founded on the divine promise. As an effect of justification, believers are freed from self-centered concern and enabled to redirect their affections to God and others.

Worship in Lutheran churches consists of preaching and sacrament, incorporating the principal prayers of the ancient Mass but with the emphasis shifted from sacrifice to thanksgiving. Lutherans observe two sacraments, Baptism plus the Lord's Supper, the latter incorporating confession and absolution. Confirmation, ordination, marriage, and burial are also Lutheran rites but not considered to be directly instituted by Christ. Music historically has played an important role in Lutheran worship, with hymns conveying the gospel message and encouraging popular participation in worship.

METHODIST

John Wesley, who inspired Methodism, was an Anglican priest born in 1703. After an unsuccessful ministry with his brother, Charles, in Georgia, he returned to England conscious of what he considered insufficient faith. In 1738 both brothers had separate experiences in which (in John's words) they felt their "heart strangely warmed," and "felt I did trust in Christ, Christ alone, for salvation; and an assurance was given me that he had taken away my sins, even mine, and saved me from the law of sin and death."

Soon afterwards John Wesley began a ministry to impoverished coal miners near Bristol, undertaking a lifelong mission to carry the message of God's personal love to those who lacked education and the respect of society, lived in poverty, and worked in miserable circumstances. He preached that believers can be assured of their salvation and, by the power of the Spirit, become capable of perfect love for God and one another. During Wesley's lifetime Methodists formed a "Society" within the Church of England, but four years after Wesley's death Methodism developed from a society into a church, governed by an annual conference.

Methodism was introduced to America by immigrants from Ireland who had been converted by John Wesley. By 1784 the Methodist Episcopal Church regarded itself as autonomous in the new nation. During the next half century Methodist circuit riders preached in simple terms to the people extending the American frontier. In their wake they founded schools and colleges in new communities across the nation. In 1968 the Evangelical United Brethren Church united with the Methodist Church to form the United Methodist Church.

All Methodist churches hold to Scripture and to historic creeds, but they do not insist stringently on detailed doctrinal conformity or profess great interest in theological speculation. Rather, they emphasize the power of the Holy Spirit to confirm the faith of the believer and transform his or her personal life. The heart of religion according to Methodism is one's personal relationship with God which finds expression in a concern for the poor and underprivileged. Worship is a mixture of fixed and spontaneous activity with even greater latitude in nonliturgical services. Hymns are prominent including those of Wesley himself. Methodism in America has episcopal organization with bishops elected by Jurisdictional Conferences.

PRESBYTERIAN

Presbyterianism is the prevailing American expression of the Reformed faith which with Anglicanism and Lutheranism was one of the three major movements of classical Protestantism. Earlier in our nation's history this tradition was represented by the Dutch and German Reformed churches and by the Puritans. During the eighteenth-century's "Great Awakening" Calvinist preachers such as Jonathan Edwards inspired an evangelical, revivalist fervor that was absorbed by other mainstream Protestant churches.

Presbyterianism takes its name from a collegiate style of church government by pastors and lay leaders who are known as presbyters or elders. The name was applied by the Scottish reformer John Knox. To Luther's doctrine of justification by faith alone Reformed Christians added the principle "to God alone the glory," thus imposing strict discipline and structure on the church lest it attempt to substitute for God himself. Presbyterian churches consider themselves to be the Catholic Church, reformed.

The discipline that Reformed Christians applied to their church extended to individual Christians and to the life of the new nation, which (they thought) might earn God's blessing, peace, and prosperity if believers led edifying lives. The Calvinistic tradition of Presbyterians holds to a dual predestination—of the faithful to God's presence and of unbelievers to damnation. John Calvin himself found this double teaching repugnant but necessary to uphold God's prerogatives.

Presbyterians believe that the faithful are lifted by the Spirit to Christ's presence in the Lord's Supper. The church is composed of the elect. Reformed Christians have been suspicious of any tradition that does not clearly coincide with Scripture, and concerned lest Communion be received by the unworthy. Presbyterian worship provides for congregational confession, preaching the Word, singing psalms and hymns, and celebrating the Lord's Supper as thanksgiving rather than sacrifice. The tradition of Reformed discipline persists in present-day Presbyterianism, which seeks to apply faith to reshape society toward justice.

FRIENDS (QUAKERS)

Friends arose in the midseventeenth century in both England and the American colonies, and consisted of Christians following an "Inward Light" or direct grasp of God without recourse to clergy, creeds, ideology, ritual, or church structure. They were vigorously persecuted by the Puritans in America, but the movement persisted and became the "Holy Experiment" that attempted (ultimately unsuccessfully) to govern Pennsylvania as a colony through faith, religious tolerance, and pacifism.

Although Friends are inward-seeking, they do not shrink from social concerns. They early opposed slavery in principle and released their own slaves by 1800. Divisions among the Friends in the nineteenth century actually invigorated the Quaker tradition and prompted a missionary movement to Africa and continental Europe.

Quakers believe in simplicity of speech and dress and

they refuse tithes and oaths. From the time of the American Revolution Friends have vigorously sponsored relief work worldwide. In 1947 the Nobel Peace Prize honored the American Friends Service Committee and its British counterpart.

Quakers hold simple meetings rather than services. Each Friend waits in silence for inspiration and, if it is forthcoming, shares it with everyone. Every Friend (or anyone for that matter) is welcome to attend any meeting anywhere.

UNITARIAN AND UNIVERSALIST

Unitarians and Universalists trace their beliefs to unorthodox views held in the ancient church which were revived during the Protestant Reformation. In 1961 the American churches of both traditions merged to form the American Unitarian Universalist Association.

Unitarians hold the ancient Arian belief that Jesus, although he is the Son of God, was a creature and neither equal with God nor eternal. For a period in the fourth and fifth centuries Arianism was favored in the Eastern Roman Empire and among the Goths. Universalists hold to a third-century view of the church father Origen that all creation would be restored to God at the end of the world. To these dual challenges orthodox Christianity upheld

Jesus' divinity, the Trinity, and the existence of heaven and hell.

Unitarianism in America developed slowly from the Congregational churches of eastern Massachusetts which rejected the revivalism of the Great Awakening in favor of a religion that stressed reason and ethics. Legal disputes left Unitarians in control of many Boston churches founded by their Puritan ancestors and in 1825 the American Unitarian Association was founded in that city. The Transcendentalist Movement after 1838 shook rationalist Unitarianism, thus adding institutional faith and social idealism.

Unitarians and Universalists have no official beliefs and display great variety. Unitarian history has steered steadily toward reason, freedom, tolerance, and inspiration, not all of it biblical. Scriptures of other religions and other inspirational literature sometimes serve as texts for Unitarian sermons or lectures. Unitarian congregations are self-governing. Baptism is typically celebrated as a simple dedication of infants and the Lord's Supper is celebrated by more traditional congregations, but only as a memorial.

EVANGELICAL AND PENTECOSTAL

Not all of Christianity is denominational. There are movements, notably Evangelicalism and Pentecostalism, that bridge and transcend the individual churches and their creeds. These deserve to be addressed in any serious discussion of the faith of Americans. The Evangelical movement is not to be confused with the universal Christian imperative to preach the Gospel to all nations and peoples. All churches sponsor domestic and foreign missions for this purpose. Christianity is not a private possession; it is designed to be shared.

But Evangelicalism (with a capital "E") is something else altogether—a fervent faith that is never complacent and always in a state of revival. It views mainstream Christianity as too often simply respectable and comfortable—staid, cerebral, and unrelated to life. Monsignor Ronald Knox, the late English Catholic, wrote a popular book about Evangelical religion and entitled it *Enthusiasm*. He was not enthusiastic about a movement so fervent about faith. But millions of Christians are.

Many Evangelicals share with much of Protestantism the belief that Christ's death and Resurrection have more significance than merely earning salvation for the individual believer. Rather, Jesus by his triumph over sin and death inaugurated the Kingdom of God. All creation has been redeemed, the universe has been transformed, and the kingdom has begun.

Other Evangelical Christians, in seeking to revive the original fervor of the earliest Christians who anticipated Jesus' second coming and the end of the world at any moment, take a different view. They are waiting for the kingdom to come. They are moved to proclaim the imminence of the kingdom and to prepare for the last days.

The Evangelical movement makes many mainstream Christians uncomfortable because of its emotionalism, and unfortunately it is not always credibly represented by tent revivalists and television evangelists. But consider this early piece of preaching:

> I will show wonders in the heavens above,
> and signs in the earth beneath—blood and
> fire and vapor of smoke. The sun shall be turned
> into darkness, and the moon into blood
> before the day of the Lord comes, that great and
> manifest day.
>
> (ACTS 2: 19–20)

This is from the mouth of the Apostle Peter, the simple fisherman to whom Jesus gave the keys to his kingdom and whom Catholics consider the first pope. The apostle goes on to predict that the Spirit will be poured out on everyone, sons and daughters will prophesy, young men will see visions, and old men will dream dreams. This is part of a speech that Peter gave on the day of Pentecost when God's Spirit came down on these ordinary men and their lives were utterly transformed.

Evangelicalism is too easily identified with fundamentalist born-again Christians who cling to a literal interpretation of the Scriptures, distrust theology, and stress individual salvation at the expense of responsibility for the society at large. This is an erroneous characterization, nor does it even begin to explain Pentecostal Christians, the fastest growing movement in Christianity worldwide. Pentecostals share many elements of belief with Evangelicals but are a distinct movement.

Harvard theologian Harvey Cox estimates that there are over 400 million Pentecostals in the world today, with adherents increasing geometrically, notably in those parts of the world with the most rapid population growth. Pentecostals also are not necessarily fundamentalists. "While fundamentalists stridently insist on the verbal inerrancy of every word in the Bible," Dr. Cox writes, "Pentecostals love the verse that says 'the letter killeth but the Spirit giveth life.' "

Pentecostals take their cue from the day when Peter and his fellow apostles were visited by the Spirit in the form of tongues of fire and were miraculously able to preach to foreigners in their own languages and to work cures. Pentecostals believe in the direct experience of the Spirit in the lives of individuals unmediated by church or gospel. Moreover, they are convinced that God will not merely save their souls but can save their bodies as well. Armed with a palpable sense of the indwelling Spirit and their often incoherent inspired speech, Pentecostals resist being marginalized. There are Pentecostal Catholics and Episcopalians. Whatever we make of them, these movements are a dramatic illustration that Christianity is as fresh, vital, and overpowering as it was two thousand years ago. For millions upon millions of men and women God is not dead, Christ is risen, the Spirit lives, and the Christian faith thrives.

QUESTIONS FOR DISCUSSION AND SELF-STUDY:

1. How do you reconcile the vitality of faith in America with the diversity and splintering of Christian denominations?

2. Contrast Catholic and Orthodox traditions with the mainstream Protestant faiths that emerged from the Reformation. Is Anglicanism successful as a "middle way"?

3. Amid the many churches, where is the one church?

4. What is the appeal of Pentecostalism?

5. In your estimation, after two thousand years, how should the Church pursue its perennial mission to preach to all nations?

CHAPTER 13

TEN REASONS FOR RELUCTANCE AND TEN REASONS FOR OVERCOMING THEM

The reluctant Christian has gotten this far and now must make a move. I can't do it for you. Not even God can. Thirty-day-satisfaction-guaranteed-or-money-back trials do not apply. You must decide not only to test the waters but to plunge into faith. Do not worry that you will thereby become a brainwashed zombie for life. We are dealing with faith, not certainty, and reluctance will always tug at you, as it does every other man or woman of faith.

But let's at least be done with the most common reasons for reluctance because they will nag at you until they are dealt with:

1. If Christians can't agree among themselves, how can I be confident of my faith?

Conflict among Christians is less pervasive than often advertised. In fact, Christians of all shapes and forms display remarkable agreement, not only about what they believe but about what is expected of their behavior. Christianity is, after all, a faith of Creed, church, and Bible. These are solid foundations for everyone who professes to be a Christian.

Christians diverge in style, in spirit, and in priorities—but very little in substance. The quiet austerity of the Quaker meeting house may seem nothing like the literal quaking of an evangelical revival, but they possess the same Creed, read the same Bible, look to the same Savior, and worship as an extended family, which is the church. Incense, bells, and statues make a Catholic feel at home in church. Other Christians find them distracting. Look at the differences among Christians as the style of clothes we choose to wear. Underneath we all look pretty much the same, but clothes are necessary. We must clothe our faith with worship, service, and community. That results in diversity.

I do not minimize the importance of style. Style is not the same as fickle fashion but more like a difference of culture. You need to find a church home that helps you grow in Christ and in service to others. Do not be discouraged at the range of choices. They are signs of richness in the landscape of faith.

2. I'd like to believe in God, but God's existence can't be proved.

When I was in college I lost the faith of my childhood and painfully searched for reasons to restore my confidence in God's existence—this time as an adult. Accordingly, I went to the philosophers and theologians (not all of them Christian) who argued—on the basis of design or contingency or the nature of being itself—that there must be a God. These arguments were superficially convincing, but they did not satisfy me, because they pointed to a perfect Supreme Being or Prime Mover—an abstract, mechanistic deity—when I wanted my faith restored in a God who cared so much that he sent his Son to die for us.

After years of search, I finally gave up looking for the God of logic when I realized that my personal "proof" of his existence was that I kept chasing him and was miserable when I doubted him. At length I capitulated to the fact that we do not prove God's existence; he affirms ours. All the time I was pursuing God he was pursuing me. He is chasing you, too. Slow down and let yourself be caught.

3. The clergy are hucksters and churchgoers are pious hypocrites.

Lincoln had it right when he affirmed that you can fool all of the people some of the time, and some of the people all of the time—but not all of the people all of the time. It's convenient to view organized religion as a big business prone to corruption. But in fact the church is more like a worldwide cottage industry made up of families of Christians who gather in community churches to worship and try to do some good for their fellowman. There will always be credulous Christians but they probably believe in the tooth fairy as well. Except for TV evangelists who have to raise large sums simply to purchase air time, Christian clergy are modestly compensated for what is a consuming life of service. There are some crooks and seducers among them, but they are eventually nailed for not practicing what they preach. The reluctant Christian is frankly more vulnerable to boring preachers and indifferent believers than to hucksters and hypocrites. So find a church and a priest or minister that challenges you and puts fire in your faith and love in your heart.

4. Church isn't for me because I'm not a joiner.

For me an idyllic way to spend a Sunday in New York is to purchase a five-pound *New York Times* and graze over its hundreds of pages all day long. At the end of a quiet Sunday I am rested, sated, and able to pretend that I am now a master of current events. Of course, I am just kidding myself. On my lazy Sunday I have not connected with the world I have read about. I have purposely avoided society. I have done nothing decisive.

No man—or woman—is an island. We are all connected. And it is God's fashion to deal with his creatures corporately. He did this with the Jews, then the Gentiles. Where God deals with individuals in the Bible it is always with a purpose that looks beyond the individual to the group. God dealt with Abraham as father of his people, with Moses and David as leaders of the nation, with Jesus his Son as Redeemer of mankind, with Peter as father of his church.

Christians worship and serve together in community. The choice of church and congregation is up to you. You will be made welcome. Look until you find a church that teaches you, inspires you to worship, calls you to service, and serves as an extended family for you. But don't try to go the route of faith alone. You will wind up talking to yourself instead of to God.

5. I want to leave my options open.

If we were to take this position about food, we would starve to death. Leaving options open means having nothing and doing nothing. Remember that we do not choose God; he has already chosen us. All we need do is accept the fact.

Reluctant Christians often choose not to raise their children in a faith. "I don't want to prejudice them," they say. "Let them be free to decide when they grow up." But keeping religion out of your home denies your children something meaningful that they may never pick up later on. If you haven't learned to swim or dance or ride a bicycle as a child, you are not likely to start as an adult.

Trust children to be natural rebels. They turn against tradition to test it. Better that they rebel against a childish faith and revise their beliefs as adults than to be deprived of faith altogether through ignorance.

6. There is truth in all religions.

That commonplace statement may be true in some ways, but what confidence will you have in a dish that you create following a recipe for combining a cup of Islam with a sprinkle of Judaism, a dollop of Buddhism, a measure of Christianity, and a tablespoon of Hinduism? What do you get when you try to make your own religion? In all likelihood you will end with a sentimental mishmash masquerading as the wisdom of the ages.

It is more accurate to affirm that there is much in common among the great faiths. The religious impulse and the moral impulse are common to all human beings. But to be vital a faith must be whole. Christianity may lack attractive features of other world faiths, but it hangs together. You can't give your assent to many faiths simultaneously any more than you can pledge your heart to many lovers at the same time. You must choose.

7. If God wants me to believe in him, let him tell me so.

He has already told you so through the Bible, through the church, and through the hundreds of millions of men and women who try each day to do God's will. God has never ceased to reveal himself through history—never hiding, always seeking and inviting. If you insist on a personal invitation consider that God sent his Son in person for this very purpose and that Jesus was rejected by many and murdered for his efforts.

8. Christians persecute one another. Why should I join people who fail to practice the love they preach?

Historically Christians have persecuted one another more often out of conviction than cruelty or hatred. Protestants and Catholics fought to make their antagonists see the light—because they believed the truth matters and that they had it. In Northern Ireland they are still at war. The violence that stems from religious conviction is not to be condoned but it deserves to be understood. Marriages break up more often from thwarted passion than from indifference. Religious persons, just like lovers and patriots, can become fanatical and intolerant. But that is no excuse for ridding the world of faith or love or patriotism.

There is nothing magical about Christianity. Belief does not instantly translate into action. We are always letting

God, each other, and ourselves down. Look upon the church as a very large club—not especially discriminating, certainly not exclusive. Jesus welcomes everyone; that's the point. So we cannot expect everyone to be on his best behavior.

9. What if faith in God is just a pipedream?

Three centuries ago the philosopher Blaise Pascal attempted to answer this question with a "wager" that goes like this: If you believe in God and there is indeed a God, you win eternal happiness. On the other hand, if you believe in God and he turns out to be a myth, you lose nothing. But if you reject belief in God, and he exists, then you lose for all eternity. Conclusion: the only losers are those who reject God.

Gambling on God has never attracted me. It assumes that the object of faith is to cash in on an eternal payoff. Moreover, Pascal's wager assumes that God punishes people who, for whatever reason, lack faith. That will not do either. But give Pascal his due. He was writing at a time when Christian living involved great sacrifices and when those who turned from religion did so to pursue lives of sensuality and corruption. Pascal was simply reassuring people who believed in God that they should bet on doing God's will.

Let's take the worst case scenario. Suppose when your life ends that's all there is. First off, you won't realize the loss because there will no longer be a "you" to experience it. Granted, that does not justify your having lived a life of self-deception. But look at it this way: believing and loving as a Christian is its own reward. It is a good, wise, and sane way to pass through life. You are not likely to have your life on earth shortened by being persecuted and martyred for your faith. On the other hand, you will have the satisfaction of living a responsible, directed life of love and service.

I do not expect to lose Pascal's wager, but my Christian faith is not just a bet on an afterlife. Rather, I am betting on a God who sent his Son to live this life with us and to transform you and me in the process. That is no pipedream.

10. What if Christianity fails to make me happy?

The Gospels tell us that Jesus wept. They do not tell us whether he ever laughed. I suspect he did, not necessarily from joy, but from recognizing, better than we, life's absurdities. After all, that is where humor and laughter originate. Who better than God can grasp the contradictions in his creatures and the tragedies of everyday existence?

If Christianity makes you happy, all well and good, but pleasure is not its purpose and Christians do not fare notably better than anyone else in the rough and tumble of life. What faith confers is confidence, direction, integrity, realization of one's worth in God's mind, a sense of being at home with the universe, and an impulse toward love and service.

If that is not happiness, it is still plenty. I wish it for you and I pray that you will overcome your reluctance and embrace the God who made you, loves you, and is prepared to transform your life if you will only let him.

Amazing grace! How sweet the sound
        That saved a wretch like me!
    I once was lost, but now am found,
        Was blind, but now I see.

APPENDICES

APPENDIX A: READING THE BIBLE

Great Bible Chapters
Great Bible Stories
Suggested Readings from the Old Testament
Suggested Readings from the Psalms
Suggested Readings from the New Testament

APPENDIX B: USING THE BIBLE

What the Bible Teaches about God
Sin and Redemption
Living in God's Family
Christian Attitudes to the Events and Crises of Life
Where to Find Help When . . .

APPENDIX C: BOOKS TO NURTURE FAITH

APPENDIX A

READING THE BIBLE

GREAT BIBLE CHAPTERS

Creation
The great epic of beginnings   *Genesis 1–3*

Ten Commandments
As important today as ever   *Exodus 20*

Moses' Farewell
Great themes of Jewish life   *Deuteronomy 31–34*

Challenge for Joshua
Stirring words of encouragement and strength   *Joshua 1*

David's Great Prayer
A prayer of praise and dedication   *1 Chronicles 29.10–19*

The Shepherd's Psalm
Most treasured of all Psalms   *Psalm 23*

Psalm of Nature
Praising God's creation   *Psalm 19*

Psalm of Praise
Answer of the sheep to the shepherd   *Psalm 100*

Psalm of Salvation
A Psalm of thankful memories   *Psalm 107*

Psalm of God's Word
For those who love God's law   *Psalm 119*

Proverbs of Wisdom
Good advice for young men and women   *Proverbs 3*

The Suffering Servant
Isaiah's prophecy of the Messiah   *Isaiah 53*

Ezekiel's Strange Vision
Wind, fire, winged creatures   *Ezekiel 1*

The Greatest Thing in the World
Paul's chapter on love   *1 Corinthians 13*

The Secrets of Happiness
The source of true contentment and courage
  Philippians 4

Great Heroes of Faith
The Bible's "Hall of Fame"   *Hebrews 11*

The City of God
A new world is coming   *Revelation 21, 22*

GREAT BIBLE STORIES

Noah Survives a Catastrophe
A major rescue operation   *Genesis 6, 7, 8*

Abraham and Isaac
Abraham's trust in God tested   *Genesis 22:1—18*

Jacob and Esau
Jacob fooled his father, but not God   *Genesis 27:1—46*

Joseph's Rise to Power
A rags to riches story   *Genesis 37—49*

A Royal Rescue for Moses
God rewards a desperate plan   *Exodus 1:7—2:10*

Exodus
A nation of slaves freed   *Exodus 7—14*

Jericho Falls
A spy story and a miraculous victory   *Joshua 5:10—6:26*

The Day the Sun Stood Still
God tips the scales   *Joshua 10*

Deborah to the Rescue
Two women show courage and determination   *Judges 4*

Gideon's Strange Army
Trumpets and lanterns for weapons   *Judges 6, 7*

Samson's Fame and Fall
Israel's strong man couldn't control women   *Judges 14–17*

Ruth and Boaz
A tender love story   *Ruth*

The Call of Samuel
A mysterious voice in the night   *1 Samuel 3*

David's Call to Destiny
God chooses the youngest son   *1 Samuel 16:1–13*

David and Goliath
A young man's faith cannot be beaten   *1 Samuel 17*

David and Jonathan
A story of undying loyalty   *1 Samuel 20*

David and Saul
Tense moments in a wilderness cave   *1 Samuel 23–24*

David and Bathsheba
Sin, tragedy, and repentance   *2 Samuel 11—12*

David and Absalom
Treachery and tragedy break a father's heart   *2 Samuel 15—18*

The Queen of Sheba
Two monarchs and their riches   *1 Kings 10*

Elijah's God Outdoes the False Prophets
Blazing finish to a long day   *1 Kings 18*

Elisha and the General
Strange cure in a dirty river   *2 Kings 5*

Josiah's Great Discovery
Housecleaning in the temple   *2 Kings 22*

Nehemiah's Dream Come True
The walls of Jerusalem rise again   *Nehemiah*

Esther's Finest Hour
A beauty contest and the king's policies   *Esther*

Job's Problems
Why do good people suffer?   *Job 1—3*

The Fiery Furnace
Three young men come out unharmed   *Daniel* 3

Daniel's Night with the Lions
The king learns new respect for Daniel's God   *Daniel* 6

Jonah's Vacation Plans Backfire
God won't take "no" for an answer   *Jonah*

Philip and the Ethiopian
African becomes a follower of Christ   *Acts* 8

Conversion of Saul
Dynamic Jewish leader stopped in his tracks   *Acts* 9

The Philippian Jailer
Earthquake almost leads to jailbreak   *Acts* 16

Paul's Shipwreck
One danger after another   *Acts* 27–28

SUGGESTED READINGS FROM THE OLD TESTAMENT

The Beginning
Genesis 1

The Fall of Man
Genesis 3

The Flood
Genesis 6–8

Abraham Tested
Genesis 22

Jacob's Dream at Bethel
Genesis 28

The Birth of Moses
Exodus 2

Moses and the Burning Bush
Exodus 3

Manna and Quail
Exodus 16

Moses and the Glory of the Lord
Exodus 33

Balaam's Donkey
Numbers 22

The Death of Moses
Deuteronomy 34

The Lord Commands Joshua
Joshua 1

Crossing the Jordan
Joshua 3

The Fall of Jericho
Joshua 5, 6

Gideon Defeats the Midianites
Judges 7

The Lord Calls Samuel
1 Samuel 3

David and Goliath
1 Samuel 17

Elijah on Mount Carmel
1 Kings 18

Benefits of Wisdom
Proverbs 3

Sayings of the Wise
Proverbs 22

The Wife of Noble Character
Proverbs 31

Remember Your Creator While Young
Ecclesiastes 11, 12

Isaiah's Commission
Isaiah 6

To Us a Child is Born
Isaiah 9

Comfort for God's People
Isaiah 40

The Suffering and Glory of the Servant
Isaiah 52, 53

Invitation to the Thirsty
Isaiah 55

Jehoiakim Burns Jeremiah's Scroll
Jeremiah 36

The Writing on the Wall
Daniel 5

Daniel in the Den of Lions
Daniel 6

SUGGESTED READINGS
FROM THE PSALMS

SUGGESTED READINGS FROM THE NEW TESTAMENT

Jesus Rides into Jerusalem
Luke 19:28–48

The Last Supper
Luke 22:1–23

A Parting Message
John 14:1–21

Jesus Arrested
Mark 14:32–56

The Trial of Jesus
Mark 15:1–20

Jesus Crucified
Luke 23:32–56

The Resurrection
Matthew 28:1–20

The Ascension
Acts 1:1–14

The Holy Spirit Comes
Acts 2:1–39

An Ethiopian Converted
Acts 8:26–40

Paul Converted
Acts 9:1–25

Paul Preaches on Mars Hill
Acts 17:16–34

Paul's Defense Before King Agrippa
Acts 26:1–29

God and Sin
Romans 1:16–32

Becoming a Christian
Romans 10:1–17

Faith, Wisdom, and Perseverance
James 1:1–18

The Last Days
2 Peter 3:1–18

**A New Heaven and a
New Earth**
Revelation 21:1–27

Jesus is Coming Soon
Revelation 22:1–21

**The Son of God
Becomes Man**
John 1:1–18

Jesus Christ is Born
Luke 2:1–20

Jesus' Childhood
Matthew 2:1–23

**Jesus Introduced by John
the Baptist**
Matthew 3:1–17

His Life's Work Begins
Luke 4:1–21

**Jesus Feeds the Five
Thousand**
Mark 6:30–56

**Jesus Heals the Sick and
Calms the Storm**
Matthew 8:1–34

The Parable of the Sower
Matthew 13:1–23

**Parables of the Kingdom of
Heaven**
Matthew 13:24–52

Parable of the Lost Son
Luke 15:11–32

Parable of the Talents
Luke 19:11–27

APPENDIX B

USING THE BIBLE

WHAT THE BIBLE TEACHES
ABOUT GOD:

The Creation Story
"In the beginning God"   *Genesis 1*

The Creation of Man
In the image of God   *Genesis 2*

A Vision of God's Holiness
"Holy, holy, holy"   *Isaiah 6*

How God Answered Job
"Where were you, Job?"   *Job 38–41*

God Without Equal
The greatness of the Creator   *Isaiah 40*

Psalm of Amazement
  "What is man?"   *Psalm* 8

SIN AND REDEMPTION:

The First Sin
  "Did God Say?"   *Genesis* 3

Psalm of Confession
  "Have mercy on me"   *Psalm* 51

God's Promise to His People
  "Because the Lord loves you"   *Deuteronomy* 7:6–8:10

The Suffering Servant
  "Are we like sheep?"   *Isaiah* 53

Nicodemus at Night
  "For God so loved the world"   *John* 3

All Have Sinned
  The answer is faith   *Romans* 3:10–25

The Importance of the Resurrection
  Is faith in vain   *1 Corinthians* 15:1–28

Redemption from the World
  Saved by God's grace   *Ephesians* 2:1–10

The Heavenly City
"Former things have passed away"   *Revelation* 21, 22

LIVING IN GOD'S FAMILY:

The Promise to Abraham
"A multitude of nations"   *Genesis* 17:1–8

God's New Covenant
Written upon their hearts   *Jeremiah* 31:31–34

The Coming of the Spirit
"He will be in you"   *John* 14:15–31

The Day of Pentecost
The birth of a church   *Acts* 2

Adopted into the Family
From slaves to sons   *Galatians* 4:1–7

David at Worship
"All is thine"   *1 Chronicles* 29:10–22

The Early Church
"Breaking bread in their homes"   *Acts* 2:41–47

Meeting Together for Worship
"Encouraging one another"   *Hebrews* 10:19–25

Command to Baptize
"Teaching and baptizing"   *Matthew* 28:16–20

Baptized into His Death
Sign of identification   *Romans* 6:1–5

The Last Supper
"This is my body"   *Matthew* 26:20–29

The Practice of Communion in the Churches
A guide to proper practice   *1 Corinthians* 11:17–34

CHRISTIAN ATTITUDES TO THE EVENTS AND CRISES OF LIFE

Adversity
Matthew 10:28–33
Philippians 4:4–7

Anger
Matthew 5:22–25
James 1:19–21

Citizenship
Matthew 22:21
Romans 12:17 to 13:14
Titus 3:1–6
1 Peter 2:13–17

Contentment
Colossians 3:16–17
Hebrews 13:5–6

Conversation
Ephesians 4:15, 20–32
2 Timothy 2:23–26

Criticism
Matthew 7:1–5
Romans 2:1–4
Romans 14:4–13

Fellowship
Acts 2:42–47
Romans 12:9–16
1 Corinthians 10:16–17
1 John 1:5–71

Forgiveness
Matthew 18:21–35
Acts 13:26–39
Ephesians 4:31–32

Friendship
John 15:12–17
James 4:4 1

Generosity
Acts 4:34–37
Acts 20:32–35
2 Corinthians 9:6–15

Gratitude
Luke 17:17–18
Colossians 3:15
1 Thessalonians 5:18

Honesty
Romans 12:17
Ephesians 4:28
1 Peter 3:10–12

Patience
James 5:7–11

Permissiveness
Romans 6:1–2, 11–14
1 Corinthians 6:9–20

Prayer
Matthew 26:38–41
Luke 18:1–8
Ephesians 6:18

Priorities
Matthew 6:33
Luke 12:15–21

Purity
2 Timothy 2:22
Titus 1:15–16

Riches
Matthew 6:24, 33
Mark 10:17–31
1 Timothy 6:7–12

Righteousness
Romans 1:16–18
Romans 3:10–26
Romans 5:1–21
Romans 6:11–23

Death
John 11:25–27
Romans 14:7–9
Philippians 1:21
1 Thessalonians 4:13–18

Discipleship
John 15:1–8
Acts 11:19–26
1 Peter 2:21–25

Diligence
Romans 12:11

Enemies
Matthew 5:10–12, 43–48

Faith
Mark 11:22–24
Romans 5:1–2
Hebrews 11:1 to 12:2

Faithfulness
Luke 19:12–26
1 Corinthians 4:1–5

Humility
Luke 22:24–27
John 13:4–17
Philippians 2:3–11
Peter 5:5–7

Jealousy
Luke 15:25–32
Galatians 5:19–26
James 3:13–18

Love
1 Corinthians 13:1–3
John 4:7–12

Marriage
Mark 10:2–12
Ephesians 5:21–33

Obedience
Matthew 7:24–29
Matthew 12:50
John 15:10–14
Acts 5:29–32

Old Age
Luke 2:25–38
Titus 2:1–6

Salvation
Romans 10:9–11
Ephesians 2:4–9
Titus 2:11–14

Steadfastness
Luke 9:51
1 Corinthians 15:57–58
Ephesians 6:10–18
1 Peter 5:8–10

Sympathy
Romans 15:1
Hebrews 13:3
James 1:27
1 Peter 3:8

Thoughts
Romans 12:3
Philippians 4:8

WHERE TO FIND HELP WHEN . . .

Afraid or Fearful
Psalm 34
Psalm 56:3, 4, 10, 11
Isaiah 41:10
Mark 4:35–41

Anxious or Worried
Psalm 46
Isaiah 43:1–3
Matthew 6:25–34
Philippians 4:6, 7

Bereaved
Psalm 23
1 Corinthians 15:51–57
1 Thessalonians 4:13–18
Revelation 22:3–5

Bitter or Critical
Psalm 731
Matthew 7:1–5
1 Corinthians 13

Choosing a Career
Proverbs 31:10–30
Matthew 19:4–6
Ephesians 5:22–33
Jude 24, 25

Faith Is Weak
Joshua 1:6–9
Matthew 8:5–13
Luke 12:22–31
Hebrews 11

Far from God
Psalm 42:5–11
Psalm 139:1–18
Acts 17:22–30

Feeling Inadequate
1 Corinthians 1:20–31
2 Corinthians 12:9, 10
Philippians 4:12, 13

Feeling Strong
Psalm 18:32–35
Romans 12:3–16

Friends Fail
Psalm 27:10–14
Psalm 41
Luke 17:3, 4
2 Timothy 4:16–18

Ill or in Pain
Psalm 103:1–4

Praying
Luke 11:1–13
Luke 18:1–14
John 14:12–14

Conscious of Sin
Psalm 51
Luke 7:36–50

Wanting Courage
John 3:16, 17
1 John 1:5–10

Sorrowful
Isaiah 53:1–6
Isaiah 61:1–3
2 Corinthians 1:3–11
Revelation 21:1–5

Successful
Deuteronomy 8:10–20

Tempted
Psalm 1
Matthew 4:1–10
1 Cor. 10:12, 13
James l:12–15

Thankful
Psalm 92:1–5
Psalm 100
Ephesians 5:18–20

Contemplating Marriage
Proverbs 31:10–30
Matthew 19:4–6
Ephesians 5:22–33

In Danger
Psalm 91
Proverbs 18:10
Mark 4:37–41

Dedicating Your Life
Joshua 24:14, 15
Matthew 16:24–26
Romans 12:1, 2

Depressed or Discouraged
Romans 8:28–29
2 Corinthians 4:8–18
Hebrews 12:1–3
Peter 4:12, 13

Doubting
Mark 9:23, 24
John 20:24–29

Failure
Psalm 77
Hebrews 4:14–16

Leaving Home
Psalm 121
Proverbs 3:1–7
Mark 10:28–30

Lonely
Psalm 23
John 14:15–21
Revelation 3:20

Needing Guidance
Psalm 32:8–10
Psalm 37:3–7, 23, 24
Isaiah 30:19–21
John 16:12, 13

Needing Peace
Isaiah 26:3, 4
John 14:27
Romans 5:1–5
Philippians 4:4–7

Needing Sleep
Psalm 4
Proverbs 3:13–26
1 Peter 5:7
2 Corinthians 12:9, 10

Troubled
Psalm 107:1–31
John 14:1–6

Weary
Psalm 116:5–14
Isaiah 40:28–31
Matthew 11:28–30
Luke 15:11–24
Acts 4:13–31
Ephesians 6:10–20

BOOKS TO NURTURE FAITH

You obviously want to start by purchasing a Bible if you do not already have one. Do not despair at the wealth of options. There are many translations of the Bible into English and each has certain distinctive qualities that you may want to ask someone who is knowledgeable to explain to you. Of the more recent translations or versions you may want to consider the *New Revised Standard Version* (1989), *The New Jerusalem Bible* (1985), or *The New International Version* (1984). If you choose a study Bible you will get not only the Bible text but also notes, outlines, and helps to assist you in understanding what you read. A Bible commentary or companion to the Bible will add still more reference information.

Below are some of the Christian classics, venerable and recent, that will provide you with a selection of the wisdom, the teaching, and the devotion of the Christian tradition. Publishers of these books are not given because in most cases many editions of the book can be found.

Augustine of Hippo (354–430) *The Confessions*
Thomas à Kempis (1380–1471) *The Imitation of Christ*
Teresa of Avila (1515–1582) *The Interior Castle*
John of the Cross (1542–1591) *Dark Night of the Soul*
C. S. Lewis (1898–1963) *Mere Christianity*
Dietrich Bonhoeffer (1906–1945) *The Cost of Discipleship*
Anne Jackson Fremantle (1909-) *The Age of Faith*

INDEX

SHARING THE FAITH

Was this book's message important to you? Regnery Publishing carries a 47-year tradition of publishing books which make a mark on the world of religion, including *The Political Writings of St. Augustine*, edited by Henry Paolucci, and *The Lord* by Romano Guardini.

To enable churches to spread the word of *Growing in Faith: A Guide for the Reluctant Christian*, Regnery Publishing is making it available at discount rates for bulk orders. Discussion groups, church bookstores, missions, and adult education classes will find *Growing in Faith* an indispensable tool for thought-provoking, meaningful discussion of Christianity.

Please order by filling in the form below. Regnery Publishing can also ship individual copies to separate addresses for an extra fee. For more information, phone (202) 546-5005.